A wise wife builds her home, but a foolish one tears it down with her hands. Proverbs 14:1

HAVE I BEEN A WISE OR A FOOLISH WIFE?

ANTHOLOGY

EBONY JEFFERSON-AUTHOR

CO-AUTHORS
SAZJANEE FORD
BREANNA PONCE
ZIPCIRIAH WASHINGTON
BRITNEY T. JONES
ANNETTE JEFFERSON
CHELSEA HAMBURG

Copyright

© 2025 by Ebony Jefferson. All rights reserved. No part of this book may be reproduced in any form without permission in writing from the publisher, except in the case of brief quotations embodied in critical articles or reviews. No part of this publication may be reproduced, stored in a retrieval system, or transmitted in any form or by any means, electronic, mechanical, recording or otherwise, without the prior written permission of the primary author. Scripture quotations are taken from the Holy Bible, New Living Translation. Printed in the United States of America

For book orders, author's appearances, inquires and interviews, contact:
details@theebonyjbrand.com

The EbonyJ Brand
Publishing Services

Serves as an umbrella for Publishing, Real Estate, Fashion, and Ministry.

For services

Contact: details@theebonyjbrand.com

Table of Contents

ACKNOWLEDGEMENTS 5

INTRODUCTION 8

Chapter 1 12

Chapter 2 27

Chapter 3 41

Chapter 4 54

Chapter 5 64

Chapter 6 76

Chapter 7 94

Chapter 8 114

Chapter 9 139

Chapter 10 151

ACKNOWLEDGEMENTS

"......I bear in my body scars from my service to Jesus." and "It was good for me to be afflicted so that I might learn your ways."

They say experience is the best teacher, but in the kingdom, wisdom is. Experience will most certainly teach you, but often times the hard way.

I must thank my Lord and Savior for bringing me out and over. I know by the markings I bear and not by defeat, that my redeemer lives!!

Had it not been for the Lord on my side, I would be lost, in dis-ease, disappointed, hopeless, suicidal, but I am whole and better. This book was birth from a place of pain, trials, and adversity. God said in His word that there would be suffering for His name's sake, but how we endure during suffering and how we remain committed to the call, our faith, and our covenant with God is what truly matters. Anyone can start a race, but can you endure to the end?

You will read in all of our chapters that grace has carried us thus far, and grace will keep us. I am so thankful and proud of each author who has written their testimonies and life lessons. We have poured our hearts out to help you avoid the pitfalls, so that you do not have to learn from experience but from the wisdom we are sharing today.

Trust me, in the words of TikTok culture, you do not have time to "find out for yourself," take the wisdom so that it does not cost you more than you ever want to pay.

It is our prayer that you gain wisdom, knowledge, and understanding from the seasons of our life that could have broken or worse, destroyed us, but God spared our lives. Know that whenever God comes to do a shaking, He also comes to restore all that has been lost. I believe that we have stepped over into a season where it's time to recover all. This book is a tool to help you wage a good warfare and reclaim what belongs to you and possess what God says is yours. I pray this book is a blessing, and may God bless each of you.

INTRODUCTION

"He who finds a wife, finds a good thing and obtains favor from the Lord." **(Proverbs 18:22)**

The man of God, who is your Godly, kingdom priest must find you as a wife. In the Bible, Esther was naturally grooming for months to be presented to the king. She had already been prepared by her uncle Mordeci spiritually because she knew the power of prayer and fasting, however, during those months in the king's courts, she needed to be prepared by the king's eunuch as a wife naturally, and she became just that.

I believe God with you that you will be a wise wife in the natural, and it's just as important that you also prepared spiritually!

It is actually better that you have the proper and necessary tools of wisdom, wise counsel, and discipline before marriage, so that your marriage is healthy, prosperous, and free from toxic behaviors that do not best serve the marriage. It is important to understand that you are not just in a natural covenant but a spiritual one, which will at some point encounter warfare. Everyone entering into marriage need to understand, when warfare comes, you must fight spiritual battles with spiritual weapons. I will go over more of this as the book progresses.

Nonetheless, it is important that each party does the necessary work that causes the marriage to be free from past trauma due to various failures, disappointments, grief, and preconceived notions.

Unspoken expectations are a killer to any form of a relationship. Where there is no clear vision or direction, it is bound for failure. This book contains Godly counsel and Godly wisdom rooted in the word of God and we have allowed the Holy Spirit to download His wisdom into this book! It is truly inspired by Him and as always, we give Him all of the glory! It's a book filled with many biblical principles to help anyone in their kingdom marriage with their kingdom spouse! Enjoy!

PLEASE DO NOT SKIP ANY CHAPTERS, THEY ARE DESIGNED FOR EVERY READER.

Chapter 1
Author- Ebony Jefferson
"GOOD VS. GOD"

"In the volumes of the books written concerning me,"
Hebrews 10:7

Several scriptures indicate that our lives and the will of God for us have already been written and mapped out. As believers, we must understand that our destinies were preordained and written before time began. (Ephesians 1:4-5). The Bible also says that the steps of a righteous man are ordered by the Lord. As believers, we have been made righteous through the atonement of Jesus Christ. Your way is set, especially when you are chosen, and it is important for you to "seek" God for His plans and align yourself to His will.

However, your destiny can be altered. Even though there is a path that was orchestrated by the Lord, our author and finisher, it is possible that an individual never come to their fullest potential in God. Here's a fact:

God is meticulous, methodical; he's very much so into the details of things. The Bible says, "Do not despise small beginnings, for the Lord rejoices to see the work begin" (Zechariah 4:10).

Everyone who is truly in the kingdom is called to serve in some capacity. Everyone has a purpose, and it is critical to know that your singleness, marriage, and even the divorce can have purpose too. All things will work together for the good.

Who you marry matters!

At some point in time, we have all heard the saying, "You can have a good idea, but is it God's idea?" In this case, are our plans the plans of God for OUR life specifically, or are they just good ideas? I am ultimately saying that you cannot afford to marry the wrong person. We serve a God who is omniscient. Meaning He is all-knowing. All means all; not half but all. We cannot say that God is omniscient and that He knows everything except who we will marry. How can we say and believe that He is, but in the same breath, say He does not know certain things? I think this is why the divorce rates are so high. Divorce rates for Christians are just as high as those of unbelievers, and that should not be. We have God's blueprint of marriage in the Bible, which is our guide, and if we are honest, for many of us, it's the last thing we do or resort to. God's word is important to implement because your life and destiny will be a reflection of who and what you marry. Marriage is not just a natural occurrence; it is also a spiritual one. God should be the deciding factor in who you marry, and if He says no, that means no.

      It is so important that you marry someone who has been handpicked to help you carry out the plans that God has for your life. Why? Because you will be a direct reflection of who you marry. The head of household is responsible for the growth and development of everything in the home. The wife is there to contribute and to help steward, but if the head is out of sync, then it can cause everything flowing from him to be out of order and proper alignment. He must have vision and understand not just his purpose but the purpose of all he is meant to steward.

Marrying the wrong person can be a complete disaster. For example, if a man is not secure, he will try to cause you, as his wife, to shrink or, worse, compete with you. Some men can be jealous of their women. Instead of seeing you as someone he is one with, he competes instead. And you have to be careful of this because if they cannot sabotage you, they will try to sabotage what you have worked for. It is a form of control, but that is how he views leadership. They must be ahead more in life than you. If you make more money than he does, he views it as a threat. This way of thinking shows that a man is not mature and not ready for marriage. Marrying can be the worst decision. The problem is, if you do not find this information out ahead of time so that you can slow things down or pause them, you will marry, and one day wake up and feel like there is a stranger in your house.

Some men who compete with you may not try to sabotage you, but they may be ok with you being sabotaged. Which is still just as dangerous because that means he is not properly covering you. He is inwardly happy that you are losing so that you do not get ahead of him. Men who have to dominate and control to get a woman to submit are not good leaders. When you lead properly, a woman will naturally submit.

Be careful of marrying a man who has shown you signs that he is intimidated by your call, anointing, and/or career. Some men can be intimidated by how others like you, gravitate to you, and call your name more than his. When a man is intimidated by you, he will always try to do things that make you shrink. He will do things to try to humble you. You can never show up as your authentic self because it exposes the insecurities and shortcomings in him. You can never affirm him enough if he is committed to thinking this way about you. This kind of behavior usually stems from rejection and/or childhood trauma. Do not internalize it, although if you stay, you will feel the pain of it. Some men cannot handle women being strong. Especially a woman in ministry. They will try to mock what God has done in you with hopes of stripping everything away that God has built in you.

I've learned that when some men see your strength, it's not always met with expectations of you being an asset to them, but as competition, it attacks their ego--flesh. This is really a spirit of pride at work in them, and it's usually paired with control and manipulation, so be careful and use discernment. Seek the Lord before committing and allow God to speak to you. Especially if you are single, fast, and pray before entering courtship and marriage. If you are already married, do the same, but pray that God destroys the spirit of pride because pride brings nothing but destruction.

God speaks through dreams!

I had a dream about a year ago (2024) of a guy I knew from college. In the dream, he came to propose to me. He had a bag that was filled with items, including a box with a wedding ring. However, instead of him giving me the wedding ring, he gave me a wristband made for a watch. This band had no actual clock on it that gave the time. I woke up confused as to why he would give me the wristband of a watch instead of the ring and why the watch had no clock on it. The Lord showed me that this relationship would only cause me to waste and lose time. Not only that, but the missing clock represented that the guy also has no discernment of the times nor seasons, as the Bible talks about with the Issachar's anointing. (1 Chronicles 12:32). The Issachar's anointing is the understanding of the times and seasons we are in. Meaning you know where, what, and how because God has revealed that season and time to you. The guy from college recently inquired about dating me (2025), but I knew to reject the invitation. The Lord was letting me know what was coming and that there is no good thing that will come from that relationship but delay and wasted time.

Warning!

I want to warn you, that although God does speak to us in our dreams, anyone in the spiritual realm can access our dreams. Hints nightmares! The times when you wake up and your heart is racing, and you are possibly sweating. The enemy can project into your dreams, and he loves to do this concerning marriage and who your spouse may potentially be. Be very careful and seek the Lord concerning your dreams because the enemy likes to bring about deception through our dreams. He plays on our subconscious thoughts and has us thinking someone is our spouse, when they may not be. Leaving you in a state of confusion, desperation, and possibly being angry with God. Why? Because **"Hope deferred makes the heart sick…" (Proverbs 13:12)** I have been there many of times and it can damage a lot. Especially a person's intimacy in worship with God causing you to not seek or worship God with your whole heart as His word requires that we must do.

If you have been in a waiting season for marriage, you know how hurtful it is when someone comes to waste your time. It is also important that you do not allow anyone to occupy time and a seat that is not theirs. This goes for both men and women. Unfortunately, waiting can be breading grounds for desperation. In this day and time, we do have to address the fact that someone else's current husband is not your ordained spouse and vice versa. There is a strong delusion among women and men now and before completely surrendering to Christ, I operated under it too. Purpose your heart and mind to not endure anymore wasted time. Your body is your temple and allow God to teach you how to honor it.

Your time of singleness is too important; it is a time of preparation, as we see in the life and book of Esther. In the kingdom, it is better to court with the intention of marriage as opposed to randomly dating. We will talk more about this in the chapter, "The Wait."

God's order of marriage has been clearly outlined in Genesis 2 with Adam and Eve. I know culture believes marriage is just a piece of paper, but in the spirit, it is a binding covenant. When God created man, He created us with 24 ribs. God did not take 5 ribs, create 5 women, and tell Adam to choose a wife. God took 1 rib, created 1 woman who the Bible says was Adam's helper, one who was suitable and compatible for Adam. Adam had no choice in the matter; God presented Eve unto Adam. (Genesis 2:22)

Again, God is meticulous; He has a well-designed plan, which is why we are encouraged throughout scripture to seek Him and lean not to our own understanding. (Proverbs 3:5-6) Now, in the book of Genesis, it outlines the origin and the design of marriage by God! God's first institution was marriage. I believe and know that He was very intentional about the order of things. Marriage is to be held in the highest regard when it comes to priority and importance. If you notice closely, there was no church, ministerial office, or titles in the beginning. God first made a covenant with Himself and man, and then man with woman. Marriage!

In **Genesis 4:1, it says, "Adam knew Eve his wife, and she conceived..."** The Hebrew meaning for "knew" here means covenant—sexual intimacy. Eve was no longer referred to as "woman," but as "wife" beyond that point. The covenant of the two becoming one flesh was done by sex. This is the biblical definition of marriage—sexual intercourse. With Adam and Eve, there was no wedding, marriage certificate, or wedding officiate; this is how the Bible defines marriage. Later on those things were put into effect that we continue to do today.

Sex is a binding covenant that should only be engaged in with a husband and wife. Sex defines that a marriage has transpired according to the Bible, both naturally and spiritually. The same Hebrew word "knew" in Genesis 4 is the same Hebrew word God uses when speaking about salvation. When you receive salvation, you are forming a covenant with God, likened unto a marriage. There are also other covenants God makes with mankind, like that of King David and his descendants. God vowed to King David that his lineage would always have a seat on the throne as long as they serve God and

Him alone. When you look at the life of David and Solemn in the book of 1 Kings 11, Solomon broke the covenant that God made with his father, David. How? By marrying ungodly women who worshipped idol gods. God forbids us to marry ungodly believers who worship idol gods.

David and Solomon were known to have hundreds of wives and concubines in the Bible. Although several wives are not God's design or will, the number of wives Solomon had is not as significant here as the point of them being ungodly and serving other gods. God warned His people not to marry the ungodly nor serve other gods, but Solomon did, and the Bible says he broke the covenant God made with David. (Deuteronomy 7:3-4, Exodus 34:16, and 1 Kings 11:2) You are not just having fun when you are casually having sex; you are forming covenants. Sin breaks the covenant with God; we have grace, but we do not have permission to habitually sin. (Hebrews 10:26)

Reflect: I want you to reflect here! This is not a reflection of condemnation. What many may think is condemnation, it is often conviction from the Holy Spirit. "There is no condemnation to those in Christ Jesus!" "You have been redeemed by the blood of the lamb!" I have to be raw and unfiltered here. I want us to break the covenant that we formed with every man or woman we have had sex with, even those who took advantage of us.

Prayer: Lord, we repent of having sex and even marrying ungodly spouses. We ask that you release us from the consequences that came with that disobedience. We ask that you break all the soul-ties, covenants, and remove the psychological hold that each man or woman has to our body, soul, and spirit that then gives satan legal rights to invade our lives with curses.

I ask you heavenly father to be set free from the hurt, pain, disappointments, lies, deception, and failures of the past. So that I can truly possess and be present in the greatest capacity as a kingdom spouse in a kingdom marriage. Forgive the sins of my maternal and paternal bloodlines up to four generations. (Exodus 34:7) Let the guilty verdict be dismissed against me in Jesus' name. I stand on your word that says there is no condemnation to those that are in Christ Jesus, amen.

IF IT'S NOT BUILDING YOUR HOME, IT'S TEARING IT DOWN!

IN THE BOOK OF ESTHER, ESTHER WAS NOT JUST A REPLACEMENT; SHE BECAME GOD'S DESIGN OF A NEW SYSTEM FOR HIS ASSIGNMENT!

I want to share with you the biblical concepts of marriage.

Chapter 2

Author-Ebony Jefferson

"BIBLICAL CONCEPTS OF MARRIAGE"

Many biblical concepts distinguish a foolish wife from a wise wife, and there certainly is a difference. The book of Ester is remarkable, and I believe that the Esthers of this generation are arising. This is not an accident; this is prophetic. So let us use the book of Esther to lay a good foundation.

Although this is a very familiar story to many, I want you to take note of a few things in that story. Vashti, who is the wife of a king. The king was hosting a royal party in his court and summoned his wife. Back then, absolutely no one could come before the king unless he sent for you, and no one could disobey the king's order, or it could result in their death. Although the king summoned her, she refused to obey and come. The officials who advised and influenced the king persuaded him to have Vashti removed. Encouraging the king to get one who is more worthy, one better than Vashti.

The Eunuchs and maids of the king's court were instructed to conduct a search. They thought they were conducting a traditional search for a new queen, but God had a much greater plan. And that plan was to save the lineage of Jesus, the Jews, and Esther was God's appointed vessel to help carry out the will of God like Mary. When there is an assignment over your life that is connected to God's plan, know that God has strategically appointed and chosen you! No one else will occupy your seat as long as you surrender and obey God. In your singleness, pray that your man of God does not marry wrong or be disobedient. Pray woman of God, that you will be at the right place at the right time like Ruth in the Bible. Pray that you will not miss your opportunity, your season, or your time.

As the Eunuchs and servants completed their search. The Bible says Esther was among the women selected to begin preparation and beauty treatments to go before the king.

This preparation typically took 12 months with the lathering and bathing of oils. The Bible described Esther as having a good figure and a beautiful face. (Esther 2:5-7 MSG) and this caused her to have favor with Hegai, the king's eunuch!! You have been fashioned already to enter into your assigned place. This was not about what Esther brought to the table, or even anything she said; the way God naturally fashioned her is what caused her to be favored. I hope you know I am not talking about beauty and a nice shape; I am talking about the hand of God and favor that rests upon our lives to fulfill God's assignment in the earth. *"Hegai liked Esther and took a special interest in her. Right off, he started her beauty treatments, ordered special food, assigned her seven personal maids from the palace, and put her and her maids in the best rooms in the harem. Esther 2:9 MSG*

Declaration: We will obtain kindness, favor, and speed for preparation to enter the king's palace.

"Now, when the turn came for Esther, she requested nothing but what Hegai, the king's eunuch, the custodian of the women, advised. And Esther obtained favor in the sight of all who saw her." (Esther 2:15 NKJV)

Prayer: We pray for divine help, destiny helpers—aid, and assistance. We thank you for provision, home, and protection. Send those who will advise and those who have divine insight to help in obtaining favor from all who see us in Jesus' name.

The Bible says Esther went in before the king in the 10th month, before the 12-month process called Tebeth!

Declarations: This is our season of Tebeth—"goodness"—Mercy and Favor.

"The king fell in love with Esther far more than with any of his other women or any of the other virgins—he was totally smitten by her. He placed a royal crown on

her head and made her queen in place of Vashti. (Esther 2:17-18 MSG)

Prayer: May God grace us with favor from Him to obtain favor with those aligned with His will for us!!! Lord, grant us favor to be loved more than all the other women, and to obtain grace and favor in His sight. May our husband place a royal crown upon our head and make us his queen instead of another!

Then the Bible says the king gave a great banquet for all his nobles and officials—"Esther's Banquet." *He proclaimed a holiday for all the provinces and handed out gifts with royal generosity.* (Esther 2:17-18 MSG)

There will be a feast—a wedding in our honor! Amen!

Be wise, everything does not have to be revealed about your past, and some things require time. Not that you are being deceptive. Sometimes it is just not wisdom to reveal everything. You are a new creature in Christ, and old things have passed away. Especially if it serves no purpose for being revealed, shared, or exposed.

Pray for our spiritual Mordecai's! Too many women operating as Vashti when God desires for us to operate as Esther. Vashti was not submissive! She was unruly and made her own decisions without being in obedience to her husband. The Bible says, **"Submitting yourselves one to another in the fear of God. Wives, submit yourselves unto your own husbands, as unto the Lord." (Ephesians 5:21-22) "Husbands, love your wives, just as Christ loved the church and gave himself up for her" (Ephesians 5:25 NIV)**

When a man does not treat his wife with honor, gentleness, and kindness, their prayers are hindered. (1 Peter 3:7)

We see in the text that Vashti's disobedience and unwillingness to submit and honor her husband caused her to be removed from the place of honor, prestige, favor, and the kingdom. May we never dishonor our husbands, for we are prudent wives as Proverbs 19:14

declares, *"House and wealth are inherited from fathers, but a prudent wife is from the Lord."* (**Proverbs 19:14**) Prudent means wise, well-judged, judicious, sensible, insightful, economical, well-advised, but most importantly, advisable and teachable. Why? You have to have a teachable spirit.

One of the many things that has been repeated collectively among men is that they want to be respected. If you think you know everything, and you do not allow him to lead, you are not honoring and respecting him. Learn to be quiet! Be slow to speak and quick to hear. Pick your battles! Not everything requires a response or a full-on war. Instead of speaking negatively, speak well! Speak life! Be a prudent wife!

Decrees: I am a Prudent wife, understanding, wise, sensible, insightful, and PLEASANT. A wife of noble character. My husband trusts me; I greatly enrich his life. *"Who can find a virtuous and capable wife? She is more precious than rubies. Her husband can trust her, and she will greatly enrich his life. She brings him* *good, not harm, all the days of her life." Proverbs 31:10-12 NLT She gets up before dawn to prepare breakfast for her household and plan the day's work for her servant girls." Proverbs 31:11, 15* **NLT**

Shift your focus!

Take your focus off your husband and place it on you and God! Declare the word over your husband. Speak those things that be not as thought they were. Not in an antagonizing way, go into your secret place, and declare, **"In this same way, husbands ought to love their wives as their own bodies. He who loves his wife loves himself." (Ephesians 5:28 NIV)**

Again, God is omniscient, and you are fearfully and wonderfully made to be suitable and compatible in **every** dynamic God has foreordained for you to be in. God designed women to be multipliers, the carriers of purpose. Both spiritually and naturally, men carry seed, and women are created to receive his deposit, be fruitful, and multiply it. Our wombs are designed to incubate and bring to full term whatever the man deposits. That is why it is critical to be with a man who deposits honor, respect, gentleness, security, and all the things needed to help a marriage be successful.

Studies show that at the moment sperm enters an egg, a burst of light suddenly emerges. Life and spirit enter immediately. Women are the gate, the portal between the natural realm and the spiritual. Things can either be birthed through us or aborted by us. Similarly, you have the ability to build your home or tear it down. The choice is yours, but a wise wife builds her home, but a foolish wife tears it down.

Years ago, while married, my now ex-husband and I struggled with effective communication. There are times we thought we let things go, but inwardly they were festering and would spill out during heated arguments. In my case, I always felt like I was giving and expected to give more than I would receive, and over time, it was silently brewing in me.

However, I remember one day being at home, and my now ex-husband was running errands. I was in the bedroom, folding clothes, and began worshipping. If you know me personally, I love to worship God. The presence of God came into my home so strongly that it overtook me. I could not help but weep and cry out to Him. After I had finished, it was not more than 5 minutes later, my now ex-husband walked through the door. I heard him go into the kitchen. It was a very small apartment, so you could hear everything being said and done. I hear him instantly praying in tongues. Worshipping and praising God, as I had finished doing. He had no knowledge of this, but the same atmosphere I was just in 5 minutes before his arrival, he is now in it. I heard the Lord say, "This is what your worship has done. It has shifted the atmosphere in your home."

Out of pent-up frustration, I begin to say things like, "Well, he cannot do those things for me. He cannot create an atmosphere for me. He should be able to do those things for me, too." Because I took on that disposition, it never happened again. We argued, fought, belittled, and destroyed each other's trust from that point on until things finally ended, about 7 years later, in 2021.

Divine assignment

Your kingdom marriage is not just for social media pics, matching outfits, and getting the bag. There is a divine assignment for your kingdom marriage. In the book of 1 Samuel 1, the Bible says that Hannah could not conceive a child; she was barren, and **THE LORD** shut her womb. Year after year, she went to the temple praying for a child. She was mocked, and because Hannah was engulfed in God's presence, she was even mistaken for being drunk, but she kept petitioning God for a son. At some point in time, a new version of Hannah emerged. She realized it was time to go deeper. Hannah eventually caught the revelation and made a covenant with God. She vowed to the Lord that if He would give her a son, she would give him back to Him. I believe that is the reason why God shut Hannah's womb. Because after her vow, that is when the Bible says that Hannah conceived and gave birth to a son. God needed to use someone for His glory. He put her in a hard position to where she finally made the best decision to dedicate her miracle back to Him. He went on to become one of the greatest prophets in the Bible.

Hannah's womb was shut; I do not think we take into consideration that prophet Samuel possibly would not have been a testament in the Bible if his mother had not made a covenant with God. What if she gave up trying and believing? Started enjoying her freedom, or worse, turned away from God because she could not conceive. Her son was able to go and serve the Lord even at a young age because His mother partnered with God. Will you also partner with God in your singleness, marriage, and divorce?

Abraham was asked to sacrifice the very thing that he longed for and finally received but then was asked to kill it. Even though it was only a test, Abraham was willing. Maybe some of our prayers have not been answered because the version of who God needs us to become, so that we will not hoard the blessing, but so that it can be used for the glory of God. Could that be the reason for the delay you are experiencing? Will you partner with God? Think on these things. It could be the very thing holding up your blessing.

There is something about a praying woman, and especially a praying mother; it is your prayers that help connect heaven and earth just like your womb. Mothers do not ever stop praying for your children. You are their lifeline. There is something very significant about a praying woman that God even says, *if their husband does not honor and respect her, it hinders the husband's prayers. (1 Peter 3:7) Husbands and wives are to submit to each other. (Ephesians 5:21)*

Unspoken expectations

Unspoken expectations are silent killers in anything that involves individuals working together, and especially in marriage. *Where there is a lack of vision, the people perish. (Proverbs 29:18)* Imagine a construction crew trying to build a house and one person speaks English, the other French, another Portuguese, but no one speaks the same language, interprets, or reads other languages. You guessed it, there will be a breakdown, and it will be quick.

Nothing will effectively get accomplished when there is a lack of or the inability to effectively communicate. Even though they all have the same goal, they must work together to accomplish it. It is the same in marriage. It is impossible for a marriage to work without a vision, spoken expectations, and tools to de-escalate when conflict arises. When a person is expected to do something that they have no understanding of, it leads to conflict, frustration, and disappointment, especially in a marriage.

Chapter 3
Author-Sazjanee Ford
"THE WAIT"

But they that wait upon the Lord shall renew their strength; they shall mount up with wings as eagles; they shall run, and not be weary; and they shall walk, and not faint. Isaiah 40:31 KJV

In a world that conditions us for instant gratification, the concept of waiting for anything, let alone a spouse, seems outrageous. The thought of slowing down while everything around you are designed for optimal speed will not only feel counterintuitive, but also counterproductive. Jesus did nothing while on Earth that aligned with cultural expectations. It was as if a part of his mission was to teach His followers how to be content with being different. He emphasized an ability to move against the grain of this world, an ability that would ultimately position Him and anyone else who chose to follow Him for ultimate success. But this wasn't the world's version of success. It was success defined by the doing and completion of the will of the Father.

Jesus understood that waiting is necessary. And before you say to yourself, "Well, I'm not God," I want to show you why He was able to wait. Sure, He was all man and all God, and He was tempted in every way, yet He did not sin. Sure, He worked countless miracles that displayed His power and authority. Sure, it was His mission to save the world through the selfless act of dying on the cross for our sins, but none of those reasons are directly responsible for why He was able to wait on God.

When you translate the Hebrew word, wait, from the Bible, you don't get a definition of sitting passively, hoping for something good to come your way. In fact, it's the exact opposite of that. The word wait is defined more by a rhythm, a synchronicity of step between you and God. Taking a deeper look at waiting, you'll find that movement is required. And while that may sound easy, it's movement not at your own pace, but the pace of the Lord. Our God is all-powerful and able to do anything, so

Jesus was able to match the pace of the Father while here on Earth, but it was less about Jesus' ability to divide five loaves and two fish, and more about His consistency of prayer and communication with the Father to know what step was next and when. His pattern of communication and full synchronicity created His ability to wait. He was fully aware of when He needed to move and how fast it needed to happen.

    At the time I began my journey of waiting with God for my husband, I was ready to receive the answered prayer, but I wasn't ready to be in sync with God's rhythm. I was more interested in the outcome and the relationship that was to come, rather than understanding the pace of God and how He wanted things to happen. Because of this, I ended up moving without the Lord and encountering two men who were not my husband, fully disguised as men of God, and more specifically disguised as *my man of God.*

    Nothing will force you to become in sync with God quicker than a counterfeit sent straight from hell. A counterfeit man or woman is the same thing as counterfeit money. They look like the real thing, feel like the real thing, and can do what the real thing does until it is tested. Until it is held under the light, but it will eventually be exposed for not being the real thing. I had been praying consistently, asking God to send my husband, and I made a vow not to have sex before marriage and take on a purity mindset where God could reset my entire sexual nature. This meant no more porn, no more masturbation, and absolutely no more premarital sex. And while I know God was pleased with this sacrifice, the enemy also wanted to test the commitment of my choices.

    Most counterfeits are agents of satan. This might seem dramatic to say, but when you decide to break generational curses and give God glory, the devil will come for you with all he has. This counterfeit was handsome and even spoke with a British accent. It took this small-town American-born girl right off her game. The very first day we met, within 10 minutes of speaking, he asked me on a date. This is where the meaning of waiting comes into play. I was not looking for the rhythm of God; I was eager and excited to be seen, noticed, and desired. I assumed his boldness was a sign that he was from the Lord. He came off as a man who knew what he wanted, and the truth was he did know. But what he wanted was not good or anything close to the desires I had for marriage.

My lack of synchronicity put me in a vulnerable position. I agreed to go out with him. When he insisted that this date be the first night we met, I should have taken it as a red flag. I forgot that the moment you say yes to the wait, is the moment satan executes his plans to knock you out of that rhythm. The goal of this first counterfeit was to get me to abandon God's timeline, even if it was as simple as a date that was never ordained by God.

That night we went out, ate at a restaurant, and before I knew it, we were back at his apartment. I not only abandoned the rhythm of God, but I put myself in an environment where waiting was not welcomed. This man had a studio apartment, which meant the bedroom doubled as the living room. As I sat on the corner of his mattress, I could sense I was not where I should be. The Holy Spirit was nudging me, informing me that I had stepped out of sync with the Father and into a dance with the devil. Counterfeit one came around the corner from the bathroom, and he was completely undressed down to his boxers. He quickly climbed onto the bed and immediately started to advance towards me. I tried my best to communicate that this is not what I came for, but he was not hearing any of it. What started out as a date quickly turned into danger. His advances shifted into assaulting, and it took all my strength and power to escape that apartment without becoming a victim of his intentions.

    As I raced to my car, I wept. I wept because I knew I had walked right into a trap. Unfortunately, satan set the bait, and I took it. My heart was overwhelmed with conviction, repentance, and sadness. I begged God to put me back in alignment with Him. That night, I learned that God's pace is not just about closeness or obedience, it's also about safety. Proverbs 18:10 took on a whole new meaning.

"The name of the Lord is a strong tower; the righteous run to it and are safe."

I had left the safety of Him to try and get closer to a promise that only God could bring in the first place. It was a foolish choice, but it was a lesson God allowed me to learn. After an encounter like that, one would think I would be stuck to the Lord like glue, and for a good amount of time, I was. We were in lock step, and the rhythm of the Lord was where I was. The enemy knew he could not come at me the same way, so he didn't. This time around, it wasn't a speed move; it was the exact opposite. Counterfeit number two had an assignment that moved very slowly. We started dating, and I was clear: no sex until marriage. He agreed, and although he never pushed sex on me, he was constantly tempting me to engage in sexually influenced moments of cuddling, kissing, and touching. When I say things moved slowly, I mean we had dated for months, and he never even hinted at making me his girlfriend, let alone his wife. It took me a while to catch on, but the enemy's new plot was a plan to waste my time, and it worked. I had stepped out of pace with God again. Counterfeit number two caused me to step into an agreement of delay. I stopped waiting for God and started waiting for him to pick me. Waiting for him to make me his wife, but that was never his intention.

Waiting with God is not just guaranteed safety; it's guaranteed intentions. God is not a man that he should lie, and when He speaks something and declares a breakthrough over your life, it is not a maybe, it's a guarantee. It was after two failures on my waiting journey that I learned this. After counterfeit number two, I was all set. I sprinted back to God! I was so done with being hurt and wrong. I was tired of stepping out of the wait and into a fire that was never intended for me. I was determined to commit myself to God's way and truly wait with the Lord.

This recommitment required fasting and praying. It required accountability and a renewed sense of faith. Once I was ready to do all these things, I began to feel my strength rise. As the Bible says, I was mounting on the wings of eagles, and this time I would run and not grow weary. This recommitment was a decision I first vowed to myself and then to the Lord. I was serious and determined to stay in lock step with God. What made this time different was my posture. I was no longer waiting on God while looking for the man to come. I was waiting with God while keeping my eyes fixed on Jesus. It's hard to be distracted when your eyes are fixed on the savior, and that's where I was.

Three months passed, and I began to hear God speak in my prayer time about a husband. It was the first time that He brought up my husband, and I was ready to listen.

He spoke preparation over me and placed a sense of anticipation in my heart that I had never felt before. As someone who could have made wiser decisions during her waiting journey, I can now understand the difference between eagerness and anticipation. I was once eager, trying to obtain something I wanted ahead of time, versus the anticipation of something I wanted that was going to be given to me at the appointed time. The week I began to feel the anticipation rise, I was planning on attending a wedding as a plus-one to a member of the bride's squad. I did not know the bride too well, but I took the opportunity to help serve her as a step of faith and a sowing of my time in an area I was praying for myself. At the wedding, I was assigned to check in guests, and I just knew I would see my future husband walk through those doors. Well, the last guest arrived, and as hopeful as I was, it was one of the groom's elderly uncles with his wife. I took a deep breath and said a prayer in that moment. "Lord, I still trust you."

      This wedding was the first I had been to where the Holy Spirit was given room to move. They had worship during the ceremony, and prophetic words were spoken over the bride and groom. It was beautiful. As we were worshiping, I said to God, "Witnessing this has blessed my soul, and if this is all you had for me here tonight, it is more than enough."

Little did I know that God was working on something major. During the wedding setup, I had met the bride's father, who was officiating the wedding. We had a short introduction that was very pleasant. Well, that one conversation sparked a thought in his mind that would later be used for God's glory.

During the reception, the bride's father told his son, one of the groomsmen, to make his way across the room to come and talk to me, the "nice young lady" he had met earlier. The funny thing about it all is that although I checked every guest in, I did not see the bridal party come in because they were in a different part of the venue. So, this groomsman, the bride's brother, ended up taking his dad's advice and coming over to introduce himself to me. That night was the night my waiting shifted. It was no longer about waiting for God to bring my husband; it was now about waiting for "I do!"

This man knew what he wanted. He was a man who loved the Lord. He was already on his own waiting journey that he was fully committed to as well. And on top of all of that, he was determined to find his wife. No time was wasted. We exchanged numbers, and the next day, he reached out, and we began to speak. We set a date for coffee to talk more, and every weekend after that, we were together. Within two months, he did not ask me to be his girlfriend; he asked for my hand in courtship. Courting is a formal way of saying I have no desire to date you for fun; you are someone I intend to marry. I could not believe all that God was doing, but I could see that this was all a product of being in sync with the Lord. The next year, we were engaged, and we married. My life was forever changed.

We waited until marriage to kiss, we waited for intimacy and sex, we waited with God so that we would be stepping into covenant the right way, on a firm foundation that would weather any storm. Why wait? The Bible says in Psalms 11:3...

"When the foundations are being destroyed, what can the righteous do?"

If you step into premarital activities without a covenant, you destroy your foundations, and it is not solid. Meaning you are not building on the solid rock of Jesus, His way. You put your marriage in jeopardy and give the enemy legal rights to come in. Waiting was not easy, but it was so worth it. Today, Edward and I have been married for 5 years, and we have a 3-year-old son with another precious baby boy on the way.

My prayer for you, reading this, is that you surrender your will to the Lord. That you shift your heart from waiting on God to waiting with God. I pray that as you read this, your heart becomes tender to the plans God has for you and that every counterfeit plan from the enemy fails. You will walk and not faint because you will be in full rhythm with our Heavenly Father,

Amen.

Chapter 4
Author- Breanna Ponce
"NEWLY MARRIED"

I got married in just five short months. Every time I share our story of how my husband and I connected, I cannot help but laugh. He and I went to high school together, yet in God's perfect timing and divine protection, He never allowed us to be anything more than acquaintances amongst the same group of people we associated with. However, there was a version of me before marriage that could have prevented my marriage, but my life was transformed by the Lord. This is the part where God stepped into my life and reclaimed what the enemy tried to steal from me. Yes, it's the truth, the devil tried to rob the idea of me becoming a wife. So let me begin....

I was born and raised in Baytown, Texas, thirty minutes East of Houston. I was raised in a single-parent household with the help of my grandmother. Jesus was not in the picture in my upbringing. I knew of God and saw my grandmother faithfully praying morning and night with her rosary. Catholicism was a tradition, not a lifestyle in my household, and I had no model of marriage either. Mind you, my mother never married. Marriage was honestly foreign to me.

I was molested at a young age by another girl around my age. That moment definitely opened a door to promiscuity, same-sex attraction, and perversion. I never labeled myself as "bisexual." It was one of those things that if you knew, you knew. I dated both girls and boys in high school. Although I had an attraction to both sexes, I could never stay in a relationship. Maybe it had a lot to do with me focusing more on wanting to party and 'having fun.' There wasn't room for a partner unless you were willing to come along for the ride, of partying, that is.

After high school, I dealt with lust heavily. I wanted a person by the way they looked. At this point, the same-sex attraction fizzled out. I was more fixated on the way a man looked. If he was fine, I wanted him. Whether it was sober or not. I was numb to the idea of knowing what true love could possibly look like. I mean, I hung out with women who could not care less about having a boyfriend and cared more about hooking up. Not putting the blame on them, by any means, but they do say you are the sum of the five people you hang out with. Let's just say, the girls I hung out with made sure we were outside.

  I was numb to the idea that I could be in a sustainable relationship. For a long time, I was hopeless when it came to relationships. At this point, I came to the terms that all I cared to do was hook up. I genuinely believed that all I was good for was hooking up, as if that was the only version of connection I could offer. No matter how hard I tried, a wholesome relationship was out of reach for me, so I eventually tapped out on the idea that I was worthy of love. What I also did not understand was that there was a deep void in my heart, one that I was trying to fill in all the wrong ways. When I was 22, I reached a point where I wanted to change. A few years before that, I had attended a local church for a short period of time. Even though my time there was brief, a seed was planted within me that God was real. But back then, I believed that truly following the Lord and living according to the Bible felt impossible, too far out of reach for someone like me. So I slipped back into living however I wanted, choosing what felt like the 'easier' way. Yet even in wandering, God's grace held me, and just as quickly as I drifted, my years of backsliding were kept short because He never stopped pulling on my heart.

When I gave my life to Christ in 2018, I made up my mind that I was done living a life wrapped in lust. I no longer wanted to be someone's side chick or a 'friend with benefits.' I knew deep down inside that was not the life God intended for me. My heart had always longed to be a wife and a mother one day. Even though I never witnessed that kind of love growing up, the longing was there, almost as if God placed it in my heart Himself. We are definitely getting closer to the part where I talk about being newly married, but I must give these details of my life leading to my "promise from God." However, before that, even though I was saved, I slipped back into relying on my own understanding. Needless to say, I conceived and had my son in 2019. His dad and I were never meant to be together. YES, I know that may sound strange, but it's the truth. We prayed, and God made it clear that the relationship was not His will for our lives.

Okay, okay, we have arrived! After only dating my husband for only five months, we got married. Even while we were still learning about one another, God confirmed and gave us the green light. So within five months of reconnecting, we were married. I treasure the fact that God stayed true to His word. I mean,

"God is a Man that shall not lie."
(Numbers 23:19.)

Here I am, walking in the promise the Lord gave me in the very beginning. I am now a wife and not just any wife, a Godly one. But let's be honest, a Godly wife? How do I become this very wife when I did not have one modeled for me? This is when God Almighty our Father, Jesus, our Friend, and the Holy Spirit our Helper steps in. Trust me, I am still learning to call on the Lord when troubles arise within my marriage, but it's the realization that makes all the difference. Knowing that if God is out of the picture, then my goodness, we are in trouble. You've probably heard the saying, "Marriage does not complete you, it exposes you." I can raise my hand to that. When I first met my husband, it was pure bliss, butterflies, and an excitement that was unmatched. Don't get me wrong, our marriage still holds plenty of those moments, but challenges have definitely arisen. As I write this, we are actually in month eleven of our marriage. One thing the Lord has taught me heavily in year one of marriage is **LEAVE ZERO ROOM** for the enemy. The moment God is no longer the center, even when done unintentionally, it allows the enemy's voice and for our own flesh to creep into what God blessed and brought together.

"There is nothing new under the sun."

(Ecclesiastes 1:9.)

When the Lord is at the center of any relationship, His heart, alignment, and will flow right on in it. From the beginning of time, satan has made it his mission to divide marriages. The moment Eve was alone, the enemy used that to his advantage to infiltrate her mind, and nothing has changed today. When we are alone, replaying how our husbands did not agree with us or how they misunderstood us, we must ask: Where is God in those moments? Am I playing the blame game? If God is not present in our thoughts, the enemy and carnality will gladly slip in. Only heavenly wisdom can guard our hearts and guide our responses. Colossians 3:2 reminds us to *"set our minds on things above."*

Marriage is from above and sacred to God. It's God's intent for two to become one, hence why the battle against it is real. As real as the warfare may be, so are the victories!

Another important thing I am learning as a new wife is to forgive quickly. In the midst of disputes, disagreements, and misunderstandings, forgiveness becomes the bridge that leads back to peace. Can I say every single time my husband and I have had a disagreement;)(I immediately ran to forgiveness? Absolutely not, but that's exactly why I am sharing this, so we can learn and grow from our shortcomings. We cannot carry the weight of our mistakes as wives. Instead, we look back, reflect, digest, learn, and get back up. Just as King Solomon

"A righteous man falls seven times and rises up again." (Proverbs 24:16.)

Forgiveness has faithfully shifted the tone of my marriage. Choosing to forgive quickly and keep moving forward has made room for peace to settle back in. It allows gratitude to rise and shut the very doors the enemy would love to open. I love my husband deeply, and that love has to be my constant reminder when things fall short and the temptation toward bitterness tries to creep in. I remind myself that he is the very man God gave me. My husband is God's son, and if I would never speak to the Lord in a harsh way, then why would I allow myself to speak that way to my husband? Remembering this keeps my heart soft and aligned with God's heart for my marriage. No one hands us a physical handbook with all the dos and don'ts of marriage, but what God has given us is the ultimate manual for life, the Bible. I spent six years as a single mother, and then suddenly…BAM! I am married. I say "suddenly" because if you had told me about a year before the day I got married, I would be preparing to say "I do," I would have said, "wait, really?" not because I doubted God but because I never imagined how quickly He would bring the promise to pass. Yet He did. God allowed this covenant to be. He blessed it, He is with it and is continuously shaping it.

    A Godly marriage doesn't succeed by accident. It's built on surrender and selflessness. It's about submitting to God's character, choosing unconditional love, and keeping Him at the very center. So we keep fighting the good fight of faith, we must at all times resist the devil so he can flee, and we move forward with confidence in knowing that God's intentions toward our marriage and toward us are always good.

What happens when the honeymoon phase ends and needs rekindling? Eh. It happens, and when it does, we must go into a place of surrender.

Chapter 5
Author- Zipciriah Washington
"A Place of Surrender"

In February of this year, God told me during a church service that this is my season. Two days later, my husband lost his job, which I thought would help us get out of our financial crisis. Unsure of the path that we were on, I enrolled back into school. God allowed me to complete a one-year program I had left five years prior. I thought this was the beginning of something new. I had experienced a season of pain that I never wanted to experience again with my mental health and my husband's. Even in that, God told me I had to see it another way. I had to change my posture and change my response.

I took my husband losing his job to God and knew He was the source. We prayed and gave it over to Him. There was nothing we could worry about, as we had seen this season before and promised God we would not handle it like the last time. God confirmed in me that this time would not be like the last. I had solace in knowing God can be trusted. God delivered on His promise when I passed my licensure test on my first try on April 16, 2025.

"God is not a man that He should lie" (Numbers 23:19).

I was standing on the promises of God. My graduation date for my one-year Social Program was set for May 10, 2025. I was excited but knew I had to prepare for our church conference that same month. A time when adults could come together and experience God like never before. I worked from home at the time, so on Monday, my husband and I decided to go have breakfast and coffee. And boy was I in for a shock. Nothing could have prepared me for the conversation that was about to take place.

As I was sipping my coffee and eating my Chicken Florentine crepe, I heard the hard words, "I have something to tell you." I was hoping on the inside that it was something good because I knew I could not handle anything else in what was supposed to be my season. My husband proceeded to tell me he found out he had a 12-year-old son. A sigh of relief came over me because that was easy. We had only been married for what was going to be eight years on May 21. What came out next felt like a slap in the face. He informed me he found out in November, and I was only being told in May.

    I felt sick to my stomach. What could have been an easy conversation turned into anger, frustration, and hurt. Another man was rejecting me yet again, as I had already navigated rejection from my father. I yelled and screamed because I could not understand why this was kept from me. Why was this something we could not navigate? Why did you protect someone else and yourself over me? For days, I cried in disappointment.

    How could this have been my season when everything was falling apart? On one hand, I was receiving everything God promised me, but my marriage and mental health were falling apart. For days, I locked myself away from others and did not take phone calls because I could not pretend life was good. I felt defeated, let down, and disappointed. I felt like God had lied to me. What about this describes "my season?" I thought I was past this.

I knew I could not stay in this place. The Bible says..

"For we wrestle not against flesh and blood, but against principalities, against powers, against the rulers of the darkness of this world, against spiritual wickedness in high places" (Ephesians 6:12).

I knew this was not my fight and that this was spiritual. I thank God for Godly counsel, as He blessed me with a friend who prayed me out of the place I was in. I also called my EAP for couples' therapy. Prayer changes things, but what it revealed was that I needed to push harder. God wanted me to be delivered from how I respond.

As we began counseling, my therapist revealed that maybe he was scared, knowing he already felt he had let us down. We were on our way to the conference. I felt so broken that I no longer wanted to praise God. I wanted to hide under my bed and weep. Before the conference, I made up my mind that I had cried enough; surely, I had nothing left. But I was fooled.

What I began to experience felt like the stages of grief. One minute, I was in denial that we were in this place. That my husband could betray my trust in such a way made me feel like I had been sleeping next to the enemy this whole time. I was so angry and had flashbacks of the moment he told me. Reliving the moment now does not hurt, but back then, I felt an ache in my heart. If I had to explain what a broken heart felt like, I'm sure that was it. I felt embarrassed because I allowed someone to get over on me. I was bargaining, depressed, and acceptance took time.

My response in situations like this has always been very natural. So I cried. I cursed, though I had previously been delivered from it, but in anger, I did not care what was said. I got physical by throwing the remote at my husband. And in that moment of yelling and screaming about his failure to protect me, something clicked. This situation was no longer about him; it was about me.

I thank God for my sister friend; she knows who she is. When I told her, she immediately prayed and spoke life into me. I knew, besides God, that I could trust her with this information, not to judge or condemn, but to pray and give direction from the Holy Spirit, since I had nothing left to give. I will admit that at first, I was frustrated at her response because she told me to get out of my feelings. The therapist in me said, "Girl, what do you mean? That's what it is all about." However, she was right. God wanted me to understand that if I stayed in my feelings, I would not go to the next level. He was looking at my response. I wanted to come from the place of rejection, and God wanted me to lean on Him. Scripture says,

"Cast all your cares upon Him, for He cares for you" (1 Peter 5:7).

I began to live in that scripture. Each time I felt a flashback or remembered that moment, I began to pray and cast my cares on God: my emotions and my feelings. The season God was moving me to require a deeper level of Him that would require me to be in hostile places and not worry about my feelings but instead rely on the Holy Spirit as the guide and comforter. Scripture does not hold us back from having feelings or emotions, but it teaches us to give them over to God because He cares about them. I wanted my husband to care; I wanted him to understand, but God wanted what I desired from my husband, and I gave it to Him. God was requiring me to get rid of offense and flee from that rejection spirit.

In the moments of my anger, I felt like a child whose father had let her down. It was never about my husband. It was about every man who failed to protect me on earth.

But I remembered my Heavenly Father had never rejected me or let me down.

I needed to lean more into what He desired to do in me regarding that rejection spirit. I thought I was delivered from it, but all God did was expose it. He exposed another level, and how it entered through open portals, due to unknown permissions that were given with the things I had unconsciously come into agreement with. I experienced what felt like intense trauma therapy in a matter of three days with God. I learned that forgiveness does not have to take weeks; it can happen instantly. I learned that my healing depends on how I respond. I wanted to be angry, but I kept reminding myself that the Word of God says,

"Cast your cares on Him because He cares for you" (1 Peter 5:7).

I knew I had to keep telling God what I felt. It did not matter what I felt if I only told the world. I needed to surrender it to God so He could heal it. People asked me, "Did you ask all the questions? Did you get details?" But God told me I did not need details. Details would only give more room to offense. What I needed to do was pray.

Pray for myself, pray for my husband, pray for my children, and even pray for our new son.

Going through this storm may have caused me temporary pain, but what I gained made it worth it. I learned how to instantly forgive, not because of myself but because serving God in this season required me to get rid of any offense quickly and walk in a spirit of forgiveness. I did not have time to allow those things to fester. One of the hardest things I had to get over was allowing myself permission to forgive my husband.

I needed God to silence all the noise that spoke against my marriage. I learned to change how I spoke because the words that came out of my mouth and what I carried inside gave life, whether good or bad. Proverbs 18:21 says, **"Death and life are in the power of the tongue."**

I had to renounce and denounce everything I knowingly and unknowingly spoke and unconsciously agreed with that entered my marriage. God does not require us to hold people or ourselves hostage to our feelings. The Word of God says,

"Be angry and sin not" (Ephesians 4:26).

However, this can be taken out of context if we do not understand how casting our cares on God during times of anger is important. If not surrendered, it begins to breed frustration and allows the enemy to replay those moments in your mind, causing unforgiveness to build. It is best to give it over to God as soon as it comes so He can carry the weight and burden of those things. This situation pushed my prayer life to a new level. My prayers did not target my husband; they allowed God to expose what He saw in me.

This caused me to say yes on a deeper level. I will admit I said, "God, we could have talked about this and gotten to the same place." However, when you say yes, you do not get to bargain with God on how He chooses to bring you through a storm. You surrender and ask for peace through it all. Normally, I am a person who feels and leans on every emotion. Even with being a therapist and social worker, I could not rely on the norm. I had to rely on the Spirit of God to bring me through this one.

God wanted to remove the rest of that rejection spirit from me. The gift that is in me needs to be stirred up more. If God was going to use me for greater, I needed to have a new testimony of His goodness and grace. This is no tale of struggle love; this is a testimony of God's forgiveness, grace, and mercy over my life and my marriage. I would say this is not what I pictured as part of the greatest season of my life, but the place God has brought me to convinces me it has truly been a great season. I have been able to see my own fiery furnace experience, and just like the three Hebrew boys (Daniel 3:16-28), there was another image in the fire, Jesus.

I've shared my testimony, and to hear people say my reaction carried so much grace is confirmation of allowing God to be God and move in my yes. I pray this story brings someone hope and surrender in their marriage to lean into God, changing and exposing things in you to move your marriage and relationships with others. Let prayer be the foundation and know that the best is still yet to come for you. I decree our latter shall be greater in Jesus' name!

Chapter 6
Author-Britney T. Jones
"WIFE IN MINISTRY"

Becoming A Wise Wife...

I never thought I would be a wife in ministry. Honestly, I never even thought I'd marry a pastor.. That was not the picture I had envisioned when I imagined my future. I was not the girl who grew up saying, *"One day I'm going to marry a man of God and stand beside him on the front row."* **No.**

I was the girl who met a boy at twelve years old through a mutual friend and didn't think twice about it—just kids… laughing, growing, figuring life out. No prophecy. No spark. No "this-is-your-husband" moment. **But isn't that how God works?** He plants seeds in seasons where we do not even have the language for purpose yet. He hides destiny inside ordinary moments. We must be mindful that God has already aligned our steps before the foundations of the earth.

We met young. We reconnected in college between 2007 and 2010. **Still** nothing. **Still** friendship. **Still** no revelation. Truth is, I wasn't looking for him, and he wasn't looking for me. We were both looking for versions of love that matched our flesh but not the call on our lives. If we're being real — and I promised transparency — there were times we were both connected to people who did not reflect our purpose, did not honor our calling, and could not carry the weight of where God was taking us.

We were choosing comfort…not covenant.

    Emotion… not assignment.

    Flesh… not future.

And that's where Proverbs 14:1 truly hits home: **A foolish woman tears her own house down (sometimes before the house is even built) by choosing from her wounds instead of her wisdom.**

Whew!
Because that was me!

A woman learning who she was, but not yet wise enough to choose based on who she was becoming. It was not until November 2019 — almost ten years after college — that everything shifted. He reached out again, and we sat down over Vietnamese rice, and God spoke so clearly it almost startled me. Not audibly. Not dramatically, but in that deep, inner-knowing way where your spirit says, *"Pay attention. This is Me."* In that moment, my entire story — the meeting at twelve, the reconnection in college, the silence, the detours, the wrong relationships, the healing, the waiting — all of it came together like puzzle pieces that had finally found their corners.

Romans 8:28, "All things work together…"

Even the years that didn't make sense, and when I married him, I realized something I need every woman reading this to hear:

>I did not just marry a man.
>
>I married a mantle.
>
>I married a calling.

I married alignment.

And becoming a **wife in ministry** taught me quickly that there is a difference between a *wife* and a **wise wife**.

A wife loves the man.

A **wise wife** understands the mission.

A wife supports.

A **wise wife** discerns.

A wife shows up.

A **wise wife** builds.

Being married to an Executive Pastor taught me how to honor the cloth without losing my own voice. It has taught me how to support the ministry without shrinking into invisibility, and how to follow my husband as he follows God, all while still being the woman God has called *me* to be. It has not always been easy — I won't lie to you. There were days I felt unprepared. Days I felt unseen. Days I had to unlearn the world's version of marriage so I could grow into God's version of wisdom. **God never calls a woman to disappear — He calls her to partner.** And this partnership? This alignment? This becoming? It is the wisdom that builds homes, strengthens marriages, protects ministries, and shapes destinies.

The Call, The Cloth, and The Woman…
Being married to a man of God is a charge all by itself. Nobody tells you this part.
Nobody sits you down and explains that marrying a pastor is not the same as marrying a "good man."
A good man loves you, but a called man carries weight.
There is a difference. A good man brings his heart to the relationship. A called man brings his mantle. And when you marry him, you marry both.

I had to learn that the cloth he wore was not just symbolic — it was spiritual.
It came with responsibility, pressure, warfare, leadership, expectation, and grace. And God had to grow me into a woman who could stand beside the man AND honor the mantle.
That's where wisdom had to show up.

A foolish wife fights the calling on her husband's life because she's still fighting insecurity in her own, or it is not the vision that she has. A wise wife learns how to partner with God's plan instead of competing with it. And let me tell you — I had to learn that the hard way. There is a part of ministry that will stretch you. There is a part of marriage that will challenge you. And there is a part of the calling that forces you to grow in ways you did not ask for but absolutely needed. I had to learn how to honor the cloth without losing my identity. To support my husband without abandoning myself. To show up for the ministry without shrinking in the process.

Because the truth is…

Submission was never meant to silence me.
Submission was meant to align me.

And when I aligned — not just with my husband, but with God — something in my spirit unlocked. I did not lose my voice. I found it. I did not disappear. I became. Being a wife in ministry is not just about supporting his call — it's about navigating your own.

When two people are called, you do not get balance; you learn rhythm. You learn when to lean in and when to lean back. You learn when to cover and when to be carried. You learn how to protect your marriage from the pressure of ministry and protect the ministry from the emotions of marriage. There were moments I had to remind myself: **"I follow my husband as he follows God — not follow my husband instead of God."** That revelation set me free. Because a wise wife does not idolize her husband, she honors God through him. And vice versa, I cannot say I honor God but dishonor my husband, who is the head of our home.

And as you learn his rhythm — preaching, counseling, late-night calls, spiritual battles, leadership, expectations — you realize something: The enemy does not just attack the pastor. He attacks the house. He attacks the unity. He attacks the wife. We see this at the beginning of time in Genesis. It was Eve that satan tempted, knowing the influence she had on her husband to easily persuade him to step outside of the order of God. The same happened with Job's wife. She attempted to persuade Job to curse God and die.

The woman will either strengthen the home or cause it to be out of order. Because if he can break the home, he can also weaken the ministry. The effects of the setback do not just affect what goes on in the private home; it can affect the flow of the ministry as well.

There were nights we had to pray more than we talked. Days we had to choose grace over frustration. Moments we had to stop reacting and start discerning. Marriage in ministry taught me that the real battlefield is not the platform —it is the partnership. And a wise wife protects the partnership.

Transparency, Warfare, Misalignment & Lessons….

I want to be honest: I did not get here because I made all the right choices. Before God aligned us, we both dated people who did not reflect His calling or our future. People who matched our flesh, but not our destiny. People who validated our insecurities but could not carry our purpose. Dr. Eric Brown of Demonstr8 church in Houston, Tx said it best: **"Mismarrying leads to** ministry miscarriage." And that word hit me so hard it broke something in my perspective.

You cannot build a God-designed home with a flesh-led relationship. You cannot build spiritual purpose with emotional foundations. You cannot build a ministry with someone who does not have the maturity to handle warfare. I learned that alignment is not just romantic — it is spiritual survival. It is destiny protection. Its purpose insurance. And when God finally connected us — in His timing, in His order, in His alignment — I understood something: **The wait was not punishment. It was preparation.**

Becoming Your Own Woman in Ministry

Being married to a pastor did not mean I was called to stand behind him silently. It meant I was called to stand beside him confidently. God did not bring me into ministry to be invisible. He brought me into ministry to be impactful. And somewhere between launching my devotional, stepping into speaking, building "*Bestfriend in Faith*," and leading women into emotional and spiritual healing… I realized: **My husband's calling did not diminish mine — it sharpened it.** I stopped hiding behind titles and started walking in my anointing. I stopped playing small to "be supportive" and realized support does not require self-abandonment. I stopped thinking ministry meant I had to choose between wife and woman — God called me to be both. A wise wife builds with her husband while still building herself. And when BOTH partners build —purpose becomes unstoppable.

The Wisdom Toolbox:

What Every Wife (Wife-to-Be) Must Carry!

Before we go any further, let me put on my *teacher hat* for a moment. Because you have heard my story, you have seen the journey, you have witnessed the becoming, but now I need to give you something you can chew on. I believe wisdom is not just spiritual — it is practical. It's applied. It's lived. It shows up in the choices you make, the conversations you hold, the boundaries you steward, and the posture you maintain when life gets loud.

A wise wife is not wise because she married well. She's wise because she **builds well**.

 And building takes tools.

 Intentional tools.

 Spiritual tools.

 Emotional tools.

 Communication tools.

Tools that help you show up in your marriage *and* show up in your calling without losing yourself in the process.

 When Your Calling Meets His Calling….

Being a wife in ministry requires more than love — it requires skill.

 Wisdom is a skill.

 Submission is a skill.

 Discernment is a skill.

 Partnership is a skill.

And wise wives are intentional about cultivating them. So, for the woman reading this who is preparing, becoming, rebuilding, or navigating her own ministry marriage, let me share the tools that changed my life. Not because I mastered them perfectly, but because these tools matured me prayerfully.

1. The Tool of Discernment: Don't marry chemistry — marry calling.

Your emotions can make you happy.

Your destiny alignment will make you whole.

You need clarity more than butterflies.

2. The Tool of Collaboration: Don't compete with the ministry — complete the mission.

Your partnership is your superpower.

Your unity is your anointing.

Your agreement is your warfare.

3. The Tool of Sacred Boundaries: Protect your home at all costs.

Your house is your first sanctuary.

Your marriage is your first ministry.

Everything else flows from there.

4. The Tool of Alignment: Submission is not silence — submission is a strategy.

It means walking in God's order, not losing your identity. It means following wisdom, not shrinking in fear.

5. The Tool of Identity: Your voice still matters.

You are not an accessory to his calling. You are an answer to it.

Your wisdom, your insight, your presence — they have spiritual weight.

6. The Tool of Emotional Regulation: Pray more than you react.

Ministry brings warfare.

Marriage brings triggers.

Wisdom brings self-control.

7. The Tool of Selfhood: Don't lose YOU while loving him.

Listen…One of the greatest deceptions women face — especially wives in ministry — is the silent pressure to disappear. To shrink. To mute. To fold ourselves into the background of his calling and call it "submission."

But hear me clearly: God did not ask you to lose yourself to love your husband. He asked you to bring your FULL self into covenant. Your husband does not need a shadow —he needs a partner. A woman who knows who she is. A woman who carries her own oil. A woman who can pray, discern, build, and stand. Selfhood is sacred. Identity is spiritual. Purpose is holy. A wise wife understands. "I am not here to disappear. I am here to contribute." You can follow your husband AND follow God. You can honor his mantle AND walk in yours. You can support the mission AND still honor your individuality. Your husband's calling is not your cage — it's his assignment that you have been graced to help him steward. And your identity should be a gift to the marriage, not a threat.

A foolish wife becomes whoever the moment demands. A wise wife remains who God designed her to be while being flexible to God's needs. Selfhood is not selfish. Selfhood is stewardship. And when you show up as the woman God created — whole, wise, anchored, and aware —your marriage becomes stronger, not smaller. You do not weaken the home by being fully you. You strengthen it.

In Her Wisdom Era. There came a point in my journey where I realized: I was not just learning wisdom — **I was learning how to operate in it.** Wisdom was not something I necessarily prayed for. Wisdom was something God *instilled* in me. Piece by piece. Battle by battle.Yes by yes. And as the years unfolded — 2023, 2024, 2025 — something shifted. I did not just grow older, I grew anchored. Anchored in identity. Anchored in partnership. Anchored in calling. Anchored in God's order. This is when Proverbs 14:1 stopped being a scripture and became a *strategy*.

A wise woman does not just build her home —**she understands God, and only God is the foundation that she is built ON.** Wisdom taught me where to stand and where to stay silent. Where to fight, and where to surrender. When to lead, and where to follow. Wisdom taught me that you cannot build a God-designed marriage with flesh-led tools. You need revelation. You need maturity. You need alignment. You need discernment. This is my **Wisdom Era** —not because everything is perfect, but because everything has purpose. This era did not make me flawless. It made me fortified. And a fortified woman?

>She is dangerous to the enemy.

>Unshakeable in her home.

>Unmovable in her identity.

This era did not just teach me wisdom —**it taught me how to walk in it.** If my story teaches you anything, let it teach you this:

>**Wives are celebrated.**

>**Wise wives are trusted.**

>**Foolish wives react.**

>**Wise wives respond to God.**

>**Foolish wives tear down.**

>**Wise wives build up.**

I did not become a wise wife because life was kind to me. I became wise because God BUILT me. Brick by brick. Truth by truth. Surrender by surrender. He built me in silence. He built me in waiting. He built me in disappointment. He built me in rediscovery. He built me in the moments where I felt unseen. He built me in the places where foolishness tried to win, but wisdom stood up. And now — now I stand as a woman who can say confidently:

I was not just made for marriage. I was made for partnership and purpose. Marriage did not complete me — it revealed the woman God had been forming all along. Wisdom did not just save my home — **it saved my calling**. It aligned my steps. It strengthened my voice. It fortified my spirit. It taught me how to support my husband without losing myself, and how to carry the mantle without dropping my identity.

My Prayer Over Every Woman Reading This:
Father, stir up wisdom in her.

Make her steady.

Make her anchored.

Make her discerning.

Make her bold.

Make her surrendered.

Make her sensitive to Your voice and confident in her own.

Teach her how to build what You give her with grace, courage, maturity, and spiritual authority.

Make her a woman who does not just SAY yes to marriage —but says yes to **wisdom.**

My Declaration as a Wise Wife:

I am built, not broken.

I am aligned, not anxious.

I am rooted, not restless.

I am discerning, not desperate.

I am whole, not hidden.

I am wise, not wounded.

I build with God.

I partner with purpose.

I honor the mantle.

I protect the mission.

I carry the calling.

And I rise into the woman God always knew I would become.

I am a wise wife. I am a builder. And this house — this marriage — this ministry —will stand because wisdom laid the foundation. Amen.

Chapter 7
Author- Annette Jefferson
"LONGEVITY IN MARRIAGE"

By the grace of God, my husband and I have been married for 41 wonderful years. I know that is a shocking number in today's time, but the unfailing grace of God, He has kept us and continue to keep us. Together, we have raised five Godly children, three of whom are Ministers of the gospel of Jesus Christ. Our other two children have served in different capacities in the upbuilding of the kingdom of God. We thank God for our five children and thank Him for allowing us to teach them about God. We love being the teacher and preacher of God's children.

Always putting God First...

My husband and I, stand on the scripture that says, "Who God has joined together let no man put asunder" (Mark 10:9). The Bible teaches us that the two shall become one flesh, so we are no longer two but one flesh. This is extremely important because the two are not always one in a marriage. This may happen if a man does not leave his father and mother and cling to his wife as the Bible commands. (Genesis 2:24) During spiritual warfare, every marriage at some point will experience spiritual warfare; the enemy will try to come in, in hopes of dividing. When we put God first, declaring His word, we are armed and armored to stand against the wiles of the enemy. (Ephesians 6:11) So that we are not fighting each other but our real enemy, which is satan. I cannot stress it enough. You and your spouse are not enemies, but the two are to be one fighting against the real enemy.

The Bible tells us that our fight is not with flesh and blood but against principalities, against powers, against rulers of darkness in this world, against spiritual wickedness in high places. (Ephesians 6:12) Having the word of God as one of our spiritual weapons assures us, brings clarification, and helps us understand the authority we have in God.

I have experienced the difference in having a Godly marriage and an ungodly relationship. One of them is honored because of a covenant, but the other is done in the flesh with no spiritual guidance; it is not holy and acceptable unto God and can lead to toxic behaviors and outcomes.

The results of the ungodly relationships that are done in the flesh lead to hardships, financial burdens, lack of stability, and not being able to have positive expectations, causing your future to seem bleak because of the lack of trust and assurance. Putting God first in a marriage gives us peace in knowing that we have a promise in God's Word that he will lead and guide us to a great expected end. It is important to have the Holy Spirit because He convicts us in a Godly marriage. I know from experience that it is not only a blessing but the key to longevity. When we have doubts about what is expected in a Godly marriage, we have a reference that we should follow, and that is the Word of God. We do nothing without consulting God first.

The benefits of a Godly marriage are endless. We as believers get to experience God's joy in our marriage,

God's peace, God's love and passion, his understanding, and the knowledge of his purpose of being united in marriage.

Putting God first allows us to operate in wisdom that leads to conflict resolution. We do not listen to argue our point. We do not listen to just respond. It is not about who is right or who is wrong. We listen to get an understanding so that the patterns that are negatively affecting our marriage do not continue. It is not wise to see that a certain behavior or pattern is not working and continue in that manner.

Support…..

Support your spouse by showing love, affection, and participation. The promise that we made in our marriage vows, to love, honor, and obey. We are to always trust each other in times of differences. We honor each other's thoughts and opinions. Knowing that God intends for us to have his peace, we know that if we follow God's commands, we have an assurance that Godly peace will lead us. When there is a need in our spiritual walk, we know that we can go as one to God for his direction.

      We do as the word of God says. We make sure in our Godly walk that we do not go to bed angry, we resolve issues when we have disagreements, and pray about it on every level, to see what God says about it. When you decide to follow God, that also includes the husband being the leader and provider, along with all that God has, and the wife being his helper, assistant, and support in our Godly marriage.

      During my school and professional years, my husband has always been supportive of me and very encouraging of me. When I decided to go back to school, my husband was supportive of my efforts to start a new adventure, he helped to take care of the house and our children so that I could return to my career and help be financial support to our family. Because of his support, I was able to not only receive my degree but also graduate Magna Cum Laude.

He was adamant about making me feel like I was playing an important part in our marriage, with compliments and encouragement. Being the wife of a pastor and minister for many years, he is an outstanding leader in teaching, which helped to make the transition easier. In being supportive in our marriage, we have learned to encourage one another even when it seems hard. My husband leads in different areas of activities, which include areas where we are intentional in supporting one another, by praying together, studying God's Word together, and teaching God's Word. Being supportive to him also helped me in teaching, preaching, leading, and guiding our family for 41 years.

Over the years, we have learned to be supportive of one another through conflicts, trials, adversities, and hardships; however, we still remain supportive of one another. We tell each other on purpose that we mean so much to each other. We share the things in our lives that we feel are an uplift to our spirit man, as we follow the commandment of God. My husband is the head of the family, and we recognize the importance of the man of God leading, and as he follows God, we follow him. We have taught our children this promise of God, that he will never leave us nor forsake us. (Hebrews 13:5) (Deuteronomy 13:8) (Joshua 1:5) We are careful not to put one another down or act negatively toward one another, even within our thoughts— "Our thoughts matter". That is how the enemy works; oftentimes, it starts as a seed planted in the thoughts.

Positivity..

Isaiah 41:10 says, "Fear not for I am with you, be not dismayed for I am your God, I will strengthen you, I will help you, I will uphold you with my righteous right hand. This gives us the blessed assurance that God will help us in our times of need. We focus on the positive aspects of our lives as a whole and the knowledge of God's Word. This is what helps us have a positive outlook on our marriage for a continued partnership. We trust and believe the promises of God. We trust God's Word; if He said it, He will bring it to pass. Sometimes we may feel overwhelmed or abandoned, but God meets us with reassurance that the God who upheld us is holding us and we are not alone. (Joshua 1:9) We look to God in our marriage in a positive manner, remembering that God's Word declares that He will never leave us or forsake us. When we are in doubt, we refer to the promises of God. This is what lifts our spirits in our 41 years of marriage. If we be willing and obedient, we will eat the good of the land. (Isaiah 1:19) A long, healthy marriage for my husband and me is evidence to us that we are eating the good of the land. We will live with a positive outlook on life, knowing that God always causes us to triumph when we obey Him. We will continue to keep our focus as believers and keep our minds on God for many more years of a blessed marriage. (Philippians 2:5)

Expectations...

Remember that we are not perfect; we all have our different shortcomings. I stop to find out what it is that makes us unique in our marriage. God is the leader, author, and finisher of our faith. (Hebrews 112:2) There have been many times in our marriage where we have had to pray, seek God on a specific problem, regroup, stop, and set our mind, heart, and spirit in order. When we have controversies, we know that we have a helper. No matter what attack the enemy tries to throw at our marriage, we continue to seek God for the answers we need to succeed. We will continue to work toward being the best mates toward one another that God has outlined in His Word.

My expectations are to continue to support my husband and my family in keeping in obedience to God's Word. Being that I realize that I cannot change the Word of God to meet my expectations, neither can my spouse change the Word of God to his own thoughts; therefore, we do our studying, hearing, and obeying God's Word as family always. We expect God to be with us always. His Word declares in (Hebrews 13:5) that He will never leave us or forsake us. We hold this scripture as our scripture of promises, and it relates to our marriage and meeting expectations; therefore, we follow Jesus. Thank God for longevity in my husband and my marriage.

Women look for Security; men look for respect.

When my husband and I first met, it was like something new; It was a new connection, I would say. Because he was so gentle, a man who loved God, loved God's people (because he had been ministering the Word of God to other people for many years) (Ephesians 6:11) I saw in the Word of God that we are to cleave one to another, I learned at that moment that I have help, and that this help is the Word of God. I want to be just what God would have me to be. God has been so good to us in many ways; he fulfils His promises. So, my learning point began when I would search spiritual notes and scripture and pray, seeking God's face, open to love and being loved. I would and still do read my Bible, pray, hear the preached Word of God, and listen for the voice of God along with my husband. I always wanted to be a Good Wife. I felt as if He was special enough to marry, then he was special enough to be treated like he was special to me. I expected to be loved and taken care of as well. Men have different expectations, as do women. Men desire our respect-I started in our marriage things that I felt would make things easier for my husband. I love preparing meals for him that I know he has a special taste for. I would prepare those special meals, and I would place it on his plate, so that way I can place it in a unique arrangement that makes it look gourmet. I have done this for all of our 41 years of marriage. He gives me compliments, makes sure that we are supplied with things we need to maintain a peaceful, joyful, happy, God-fearing life.

    I love this security. My husband has a soft, caring heart; he puts his heart and soul into helping others, and I am here to help and assist him. I thank God that for all these years I still feel a special sense of security because he is always there to supply the needs of our family, our children, our home, that which we have been blessed to own. I appreciate the loving gestures of gifts, hugs, and loving moments, supplying our needs. He prays for us and seeks God for our needs and wants with me. God says that he would supply all of our needs according to his riches and glory. (Philippians 4:19) Because I know that my husband is old school, where a man is the head in charge, therefore he does not smile on someone just stepping in and being the leader and front-person in charge, where he is the head. That has helped me in our marriage. I am not the head of our house, so I'm perfectly alright following his lead. I have read in the Word of God that the man is the Head of the wife, and we are to submit to his leadership. (Ephesians 6:12.) And the scripture says," Ephesians 5:22 says Wives submit yourselves unto your own husband, as unto the Lord. For the husband is the head of the wife, even as Christ is the head of the church: and he is the savior of the body.

Honesty! Open-Communication! (1Corinthians 13:4-7) In any marriage, there will be issues and problems. Our forty-one years of marriage have been no different. There are no perfect marriages; however, we have learned to work through our issues and situations.

The Bible teaches us that through love and determination, we choose to endure trials, tribulations, and other obstacles in our lives, using the Word of God as our guide. Allowing time for discussions and communication concerning our problems. This has proven to be very helpful in our longevity of marriage. We make it a goal to value each other's opinion and thoughts in the matter we are discussing. We have learned that when we have these discussions, the problem at hand is not as dire as we once thought.

In Honest and Open Communication, we must be willing and open to discuss any matter concerning our relationship. There have been times when a conversation seemed like it was not going the way we had anticipated, but once we opened up honestly with our thoughts, we were able to settle our differences. Whenever there was a time that we couldn't settle our differences, we would agree to disagree and go on in love.

Our open communication has allowed our marriage to blossom in love and affection beautifully. I love the little touches, the bright smile, the warm embrace, just from the fact that we trust each other enough to show the beauty of communication.

Having tough conversations, instead of ignoring the problem (Colossians 3:13), we have made it a promise to each other to "Say it like you really mean it". We have found that when we say it straightforwardly to each other, what we said to each other is easier to work out because we both understand the other's viewpoint on what we actually mean. (Colossians 3:13). We always want to acknowledge the problem in a way that neither one of us feels belittled. Because of the special love that we feel for each other, our opinions matter in our decision-making. We listen to one another's ideas and include them in our conversations. We give God glory, and we give God praise and honor, that we have never gone so far as to hit or physically abuse each other.

We have children who play a very important part in our lives. (Ephesians 6:1) and (Colossians 3:20) Therefore, they are not eliminated from ideas and situations that may occur in our home. We look out for one another in all areas of our household. Even though they are a part of our household, they do not play a role in marital decisions. When we have marital discussions and decision-making, they are not included in the discussion unless they are asked to be included. Our discussions are private, and we handle them as adults in an adult manner. We give God glory, and we give God praise and honor, that we have never gone so far as to hit or physically abuse each other.

During our earlier years of marriage, it seemed overwhelming to have some of the tough conversations because of the feeling in ourselves that my mate would not approve of my feelings, and it would cause more chaos. After some time of this happening, I realized it was a help on both our parts to iron out our differences rather than ignore what was happening and hold it back.

We recognize in our years of marriage that ignoring the problem does not solve the problem; it only delays the problem. Having the discussion, talking out the intended solution has resulted in a positive way for our marriage. No one else can work out our problem, make our decisions, or resolve our issues as we can. We resolve issues on purpose. We help each other pinpoint marriage crises so we can resolve them together.

We have decided that we will talk out our problem from then on, because we never need nor do we want to have the problem that we ignored to resurface later on in our marriage. We have learned that when we go ahead and discuss a problem, it shows that we trust our relationship enough to have the conversation.

To ignore it can also resemble "hiding it." I would suggest keeping it fair, laying it out, and dealing with it now. This is how it has worked for us, dealing with it openly with one another. No one wants to be hurt, opening or by covering it. Thank God that we have very good thoughts and plans already laid out for a positive expected end. We share many ideas and spiritual goals for our children as they experience adulthood, as parents, husbands or wives, for a positive future.

I am so glad we have an advocate in Christ Jesus; our Father is our great example in our lives.

We are looking forward to many more years of Longevity of Our Marriage. **Never go to bed angry (Ephesians 4:26)**. The Bible states: "In your anger do not sin," "Do not let the sun go down while you are still angry, and do not give the devil a foothold." (Ephesians 4:26,27). I have heard this scripture quoted for many years, and whenever I hear it quoted, it means more and more to me. When I was young, I remember hearing my mother say this very scripture. I really did not understand the impact it had on my life. Now that I am mature, it has great meaning to me.

In a simpler way, it is saying more clearly, you do not know what could happen to you overnight that could prevent you from living to see the next day, therefore missing out on your forgiveness. As I look back on my life, I can understand ways that this scripture can land right at home. When the scripture clearly says do not let the sun go down on your wrath. It says you don't know if you will be alive to see another day of God's blessings.

I desire to always ask for forgiveness while I have a chance. My parents told me when I was a child that tomorrow is not promised to you, do not put off tomorrow, what you can do today. I never forgot this scripture, and in our marriage, we apply it to our lives today. My husband and I have made this scripture apply in our lives, both day and night. We make it a point to pray before we go to bed and also ask God to forgive us of all our sins and to cleanse us from all unrighteousness. We are forgiven for our sins. As we pray this prayer for ourselves, we also relate these prayers to our children and their children. We will live a long life praying and believing that God hears and He answers us in our marriage. My children have learned to pray and never go to bed angry.

Never Allow the Day to End-As A Christian Couple, we never will allow the day to end without being in peace with God, and peace with one another! I am thankful for our intimacy in our quiet trips, secret moments, doing what makes each other smile, being with our children, secret gifts, and passionate lifestyle; it is well worth it.

This Blessing of Marriage from our God will always see us through. Because today never stops offering and providing us with added blessings, we will continue to be in Love with God, in Love with our children, in love with our surroundings, and our marriage will continue to be grounded in God's Word. We are reaching for even higher heights in our marriage because God is our Refuge and our Fortress. We seek God always in our marriage. Our Marriage is grounded on a solid Rock, and that Rock is Jesus. Thank God for His amazing bond in our marriage!!! My husband and I see more clearly now the many things that are open in our lives if we just put God first and allow him to continue to be manifested in our lives.

Love has kept us together all these 41 years, and love will always keep us together throughout our Lifetime.

Chapter 8
Author- Chelsea Hamburg
"STARTING OVER"

If you have ever had to start over, you know exactly what I mean when I say that starting over does not feel possible in the moment, but eventually, you must face the reality that you have no other choice but to pick up the scattered pieces and begin again. You may feel like you do not have the strength, capability, or even the inspiration to step into whatever waits on the other side. It may even feel like you have lost everything you thought you had built, only to look in the mirror and realize you must be rebuilt inside out as well. I never imagined that one relationship would send my entire life into a downward spiral and push me to the point of trying to take my own life. Twice.

I never imagined I would lose everything I worked so hard for, all in such a short span of time. You know the saying: "When you hit rock bottom, the only way from there is up." When I hit mine, it felt like everything was falling apart, only to later realize that was the beginning of something new. Starting over is a PROCESS. If I could encourage anyone, including myself at that time of starting over, I would tell you this... ***Isaiah 43:19 "Do not remember the former things, nor consider the things of old. Behold, I am doing a new thing; now it springs forth, do you not perceive it? I will make a way in the wilderness, and rivers in the desert."***

This was the scripture the Lord spoke to me through His word one morning as I routinely, slowly rolled out of bed with a broken and surrendered heart. When I opened my Bible, these words met me like a bright light bringing clarity to my situation. I want to draw your attention to the phrase "I am doing…" in the scripture, which speaks in the present tense. For us, what God is doing is a process, but for God, it is already finished. In the process, I experienced days that felt unreachable, days when backwardness tried to pull me under and delay the healing process. One thing I had to remember, growing is never glamorous, and it can get ugly before it gets beautiful. My God, I experienced some dark, ugly days. There are so many emotions, private and public struggles, and identity battles that I had to go through when I decided to look ahead to grow and go forward!

Starting over is one of the most uncomfortable, unfamiliar, yet necessary seasons we will ever face. No matter how strong you are, starting over always comes with a quiet fear that produces questions like: "What if I cannot get back up? What will people say? What if I am not worthy enough to be loved by someone?" "What if the next relationship fails?" "What if I'm not ready?" These are questions the human mind tends to rehearse, and they can sometimes steer you away from starting over. So many days I would feel embarrassed, confused, worthless, or even exhausted, but I had to remind myself that starting over does not mean I failed. It means I survived what came to stop my momentum and delay my purpose from receiving God's choice for my life. Whether you are having to start over in ministry or start over in love, it does not mean God is done with you. It simply means one chapter ended and God is preparing you to walk into the next one with clearer sight, stronger wisdom, and a softer heart. Sometimes what we view as falling apart is God putting the correct pieces together. Because we often view things differently than God, we tend to look through a broken lens rather than a healed lens to perceive what the Lord is doing.

      In 2017, I was serving in the nursery at church one night when I was pursued into a relationship via social media, attracted by unhealed wounds and the pain of my daddy's issues. The relationship felt exciting, meant to be, and it just felt flat-out right. He would express that we had mutual friends, but somehow, we never crossed paths, so he said it was God's timing. Chile, I took his words and ran with them because I had been single for so long that I believed that maybe it's God's timing and God is in this connection. The persistence and attention this man gave me fed my "father wounds" and had my emotions high, yet it starved my discernment. I wanted my father to acknowledge me as his daughter and show his love towards me. So, I craved acceptance and attention, and this man gave me that, and it became my unhealthy definition of love.

One thing I have learned is that when you are desperate, you do not discern well. You want what you want and when you want it. We end up pushing the red flags and stop signs to the background. We tend to set our minds on wanting what the flesh desires and give more grace and time than what is deserved. The Lord showed me, within the same week of meeting this man, that God was not in the relationship. I remember clearly sitting outside in my car on my lunch break, talking to him, and the Lord said, "Ask him who he lives with." I did not want to seem spooky and run this guy away, so I held back.

The Lord spoke a second time, and I finally asked him, and he said he had just moved back to Louisiana, so he now lives with his sister. I left it at that, knowing God had me ask him that for a reason, but I was too wrapped up to pick up what the Lord was putting down. I ignored the warning and bypassed the YEILD sign and walked into a toxic relationship with an individual who had a narcissistic personality disorder. I did not have a clear description of what a toxic relationship looked like until I was already deeply invested in one. There are days within the process when you will feel weak, and on others, hopeful. One day, I felt like I was making progress, and the next day, I would question if it was even working. That is normal! I struggled in these areas more than a little bit, and I want to discuss later what I call in the process "celebrate small wins." It keeps you moving forward and looking forward to any small progress to celebrate and reminds you that you are still moving and alive.

Starting over does not require perfection in the process, but it does require willingness. You must be willing to put one foot forward every day and expect to rise above where you were yesterday. You must be willing to forget the former things and allow the Lord to

create something new. Most of all, you must be able to look fear in the face every day and exercise your faith and believe there is more. This is work that only you can do to experience total restoration on the other side of loss. You do not have to rebuild completely today- remember that. Be patient and show yourself grace. You have had a traumatic experience, and it is okay to take it slow and heal. ***"The race is not given to the swift nor the strong, but to the one who endures to the end. "***
Ecclesiastes 9:11

The Invasion

My childhood environment and seeing unhealthy relationships created a narrative that labeled apart of love to be acceptable when someone tries to control your emotions and your response, and that it is tough love mixed with encouragement when they verbally abuse you for the sake of them saying they love and want the best for you. What I thought was God sent was control and witchcraft sent by the enemy that was feeding on my unhealed wounds the entire time. The attention I received from him, whether good or bad in the moment, felt like love. His consistency felt like commitment, and I wanted to believe with everything in me that he cared about me, so I ignored the signs that showed evidence that he did not. He knew how to say the right things. He knew how to act interested enough to keep me attached to serve his purpose but not invested enough to truly be present. The more I gave, the less he respected me. The more I tried to express myself, the more he shut down, blamed me, or made me feel crazy for feeling anything at all. At the time, I was simply trying to love someone who was breaking me. So many things began to show up in the relationship, and certain behaviors began to multiply that made me feel smaller than I have ever felt in life.

He would say that no one wanted me but him. He would verbally abuse me in ways that broke me mentally down, where I began to lose my identity and pick up the identity of what he wanted me to be for him. He had a way of twisting my words until I felt guilty for speaking up if I called out his behavior; somehow, I became the problem. Somehow, I would be the reason he cheats, yells, shuts down, stays out, or gets angry and breaks the windows out of the house. If I cried, he said I was "too emotional." If I asked for clarity, he would say I was "doing too much." If I found the courage to set boundaries, he acted like I was attacking him and not supporting him as a man. That is one thing about narcissistic behavior: it makes you question your reality. It makes you apologize for things you did not do. It makes you shrink just to keep the peace. You shrink who you are to fit who they want you to be. You silence your voice to avoid conflict. You sacrifice your needs so theirs can stay centered. Little did I know that what I called submission was self-abandonment.

Little by little, I felt my confidence and identity slipping away, my voice got weaker, my needs became smaller. And out of all things, my prayer life began to fade. I was being stripped of my source of strength, power, and instructions in prayer. When I would go into my prayer closet at 4 am, he would get angry and tell me that God does not want me to lose sleep just to pray. At that moment, I knew I was sleeping with the enemy. I continued to get weaker the longer I stayed out of prayer. (Someone not understanding the power of prayer is something I will never be able to compromise; it is non-negotiable.) Prayer is ESSENTIAL!

I saw with my own two eyes him cheating, text messages, pictures, and received calls from other women. I began to question if I was enough of a woman not just for him but for anyone. Things he liked to do, I agreed to do to please him. I was not myself anymore; I was whoever and whatever he needed me to be in the moment while trying to chase God at the same time. Submission to the wrong person is spiritual, emotional, and mental slavery disguised as loyalty. It can damage every part of your identity, it distorts your discernment, and disconnects you from God. The wrong relationship will require you to give up everything except them. He would try to isolate me from people who could speak the truth and call out his motives.

My family, church community, and friends were labeled as not good for me. I began to miss church and dance rehearsal, all because he did not want to go to church. He became my idol; he became my god, and because I allowed this man to sit on God's throne in my heart, the Lord allowed everything to fall apart even more.

Exodus 20:3–4 You must not have any other god but me. You must not make for yourself an idol of any kind or an image of anything in the heavens or on the earth or in the sea. (NLT)

This scripture is about idolatry. It is possible to be in idolatry and not know it. Anything and anyone can become an idol if we allow it to take the place of the Holy Spirit or God. For example, people, food, jobs, pastors, etc. If you run to these things or people for comfort and solutions and not God or Him first consistently, if you only heed to their voice or lend your body to it, it has become your idol.

When Life Fell Apart

Everything began to happen so fast, and things I had worked for prior began to get snatched away. I was depressed, weak, and stressed out. I was losing my mind, weight, and sleep as time progressed. The emotional stress did not stay emotional. It started to hit every area of my life. My finances, my stability, and my mental health declined; I lost my car, my home, and my job after taking a LOA and getting counseling. I could not believe I was sitting in a counselor's office because I could not manage my life and emotions. I was a wreck. I felt like I was losing my mind while I was trying to hold on to a man who was not even holding on to me. I was trying to save a relationship that was destroying everything piece by piece.

What I have learned from this is that, when someone comes along and your life begins to decline, God did not send them. They are a counterfeit of the real thing that God has purposed for your life. Whenever we step out of the will of God, I am reminded of the story of Abraham and Sarah, that is when Ishmael is birth, but when you wait on the promise God gives us, Issac, the promise of God. God is a God of increase and multiplication. Everything flourishes in God's presence. I did not realize that sometimes God will let what you are clinging to fall apart just to keep you from losing yourself completely. After he came home late one morning, I did not let him in the house, so he broke the windows in my house. The next morning, I decided on my way to church that I was letting go. He came to the house after church, and I told him that it was over. He said he was sorry and wanted to do right. I was firm in the moment and made up in my mind that I was done. But I still had room in my heart for him to come back in case he decided to do it right. I knew I did not have the strength to move on.

This is the fruit of soul-ties. Soul-ties join the spirits of two individuals and will keep you in relationships and situationships that you should remove yourself from, but because your souls are tied by emotions, sex, and wounds, you stay. This type of bond is only meant for those in covenant, marriage. Where the two become one flesh. He later got an apartment, and I operated in a spirit of backwardness and later took him back. I went to his apartment one day after he had not answered the phone. Of course, it was someone there. After creating damage here and there, I left. When I replayed in my head the damage I caused, I was so disappointed in myself, and I never wanted to act out the way I did ever again. So, I prayed, and one day, while in prayer, I will never forget.I told God: "Lord, if he doesn't reject me, I'm going to stay and continue to be his fool." It was not a prayer of strength, but it was certainly a bold, honest prayer of humility. I knew I would be capable of going back if he showed me any sign of acceptance. Not long after that prayer, the man started dating someone else and began to reject my phone calls. It hurt me, but I knew it was my prayer being answered because I permitted God to do what He wanted. This is a prayer that you only pray when you really want God to rearrange your life completely, and you must be ready to deal with the side effects of grief from the loss.

A week later, I found out he was dating someone at his new job. I called him to confirm, and he would not pick up the phone. I felt even more hurt and rejected at this point. The rejection is what I needed because it was my protection from the trap the enemy set that was waiting to take place in the future. Even though I walked away first, it was the rejection that made me feel like I made the wrong decision. I remember after days of calling his phone and getting no answer, I began to have withdrawals and wanted to mend the relationship. I truly thank God that he never answered my call. I had already moved in with my mom after losing everything, and I could remember the mornings when I would literally slide out of bed to the floor, crying. I would have days where I look in the mirror and cry and ask God will I ever be able to smile again. I had no hope that the pain would go away. I was in the grieving stage in the process.

The enemy had me feeling like there was nothing to continue to live for. It was a morning routine that I found myself doing every morning until one morning I sat in bed while my kids were in school, and I put my bible on my lap and began to cry and tell God, "Lord, speak to me in your word like the elders said you would speak to them back in the day". Tears flowing on the cover of my bible, I open the bible and Isaiah 43:19 jumped off the pages. As I began to read the scripture, I began to cry tears of joy because the Lord heard my cry. I began to thank God for not forsaking me or leaving me in my mess after He warned me. It was the best feeling in the world to hear God speak so clearly and strongly to my spirit. That was the first day I combed my hair and put on clothes. The next morning, as I was driving to take my children to school, I heard the Lord say, "Write about it". I began to tell the Lord, I do not know how or what to say about this. The Lord said that He would show me.

    I was obedient and stepped out on faith and began to write. I wrote my first book, "Survive the Break: Rehab After Brokenness". Writing was the beginning of starting over for me because it shifted my focus to the bigger picture rather than keeping the pain on me.

Starting Over

There are so many different emotions and thoughts that we all go through in the process of starting over. This is the very reason I say to be patient with yourself and your heart. Some days you feel like you're going strong, and the next days you feel like you are back at square one. It is a sign that you are not standing still but that the spirit and flesh are at war. Heartbreak disrupts routines, creates a theory that you are not safe to love again, and it even makes you want to sleep through the pain, so you do not have to face the heaviness you feel awake. It is the worst feeling a human can experience when you have truly loved. There are practical things that can and should be done when starting over.

Prayer

Prayer is BIG! I know it was hard for me to get to a place and pray when I was all over the place. I was not feeling seen because I was being rejected by someone, I craved the acceptance from, so I felt as if God would not see me either. It was a lie from the enemy to keep me from going back into my closet and seeking God's instructions. It does not have to be a long prayer; it just needs to be real and honest. I needed guidance and instructions to start over. I prayed to God an honest prayer from my heart that I was weak and needed His strength to get me out of the mess I was in. I prayed for the Lord to speak to me the way He spoke to the elders in the bible. I prayed to God about my next step, and I did not know how to follow through on what He asked me to write. My assurance came from God, and I felt more secure with each step I took afterward. I repented and asked for forgiveness for being rebellious after He warned me from the beginning. I stayed consistent with the small moments of prayer and communion, and it gradually began to grow again.

Small Win

I live by this now because it is very encouraging to me to never forget to celebrate every small win. It does not have to be grand, big, or publicly validated to be celebrated. There are silent battles and struggles that no one will see you overcome in private, but when you do, you deserve to pat yourself on the back and celebrate it. It could be as small as putting on clothes and combing your hair. That is not easy when you do not feel pretty or desirable. If you find yourself not crying as much as you cried the week before, that is something to celebrate because of the growth. Or even getting out of bed is big! Do not allow anyone, not even yourself, to cheat you out of your small victories. A win is a win!

Denial and Disbelief

One of many emotions I had to deal with was acknowledging the loss. Denying pain or suppressing feelings can lead to long-term emotional baggage. When we deny that we are not okay, that it hurts, or that we feel the pain, we unintentionally take this baggage into the next relationship and cause others to deal with it as if they were the ones who created it. Acknowledging the loss is a major step that must be faced because you can never defeat what you will not confess exists. Admitting that it happened and that you are feeling the weight of it is important.

Identity Battles

The Lord had to really restore my entire identity, starting over. I came into agreement with so many different labels in the relationship that were put on me. Some days, I felt guilty for feeling like I deserved to be loved properly and healthy. The relationship made me feel unworthy, unwanted, abandoned, and less valuable. I tried to adjust even the outer appearance of who I was to look like the woman that he desired. Before the relationship, I was content and liked myself, but the longer I was in the relationship, the more I began to dislike myself. It was the word of God that rebuilt me with being able to identify who I was in God again, not another human or a new wig or body, but Christ's word. It's imperative to rediscover and reconnect with your own identity outside of the relationship. Sometimes we feel like, after we are no longer in a relationship, who we were in the relationship no longer exists. True enough, it does not. A new layer of who God has called forth and shaped you to become now lives intentionally and on purpose.

This is why a relationship should never determine your identity or happiness, because we can become so content with the normal and comfort that we never expect to evolve. Never lose yourself in a relationship, but make sure you find yourself before entering a relationship.

Spiritual collapse

My walk with God became shaky while in that relationship, so my relationship with Christ needed to be revived. I attended church and ministered broken while feeling unseen and disqualified. I felt like my mistakes and sins disqualified me from serving in ministry. It was bad that I battled with forgiving church leaders who said they loved me but never showed up when I needed them, yet they created stories about me. I felt alone and did not want to be a part of another church after that. Even in feeling abandoned and talked about, the Lord had to deal with all the wounds of my past so that I could walk lightly into my future. I had no idea that my brokenness and survival were what qualified me to be usable to the kingdom. I became consistent and obedient to whatever I believed the Lord would speak. I began to fall head over heels in love with God's consistency and the way He loved me. I began to love myself again.

Mental - Mind Battles

Pulling down the strongholds in my mind was the toughest part. My soul, my mind, was tied to the past emotions, feelings, laughter, and plans I created in my mind that were hard to release. I pictured the future of us together and could not erase the created images or feelings. We bonded over trauma and similar life experiences in certain areas, so I felt like detachment from the mind was a rough challenge. I had to eat the word repeatedly and think about how to identify the root and uproot it. My mind had to be renewed because it had taken some blows, and my thoughts became polluted and contaminated. I had mental meltdowns and times when I would be so disappointed with myself that I did not identify what was taking place. I had to forgive myself and give myself grace.

Lesson Learned

I now carry those lessons with a healed heart that love should never cost me my identity, my peace, or my relationship with God. I learned that honoring my own worth, listening to my discernment the first time, and refusing to shrink myself just to be loved by someone else is key. I can feel safe entering into a new relationship because I have set boundaries, communicate effectively, and allow love to grow slowly, naturally, and safely. I no longer apologize for needing healthy love. This time, I'm showing up whole and healed, and I expect the same in return. **Isaiah 43:19**

Starting over did not look like strength to me at first. It looked like weakness, low self-esteem, and a heart that did not know how to beat in a broken place. Nights where fear tried to convince me I had nothing left to live for. But look at me now! Hallelujah! What I did not know then was that God was already moving and Heaven was already holding the blueprint to start over and start NEW!

Starting over became my classroom. It taught me to sit still long enough for God to unlearn the lies I had believed and to heal the wounds that attract pain. It taught me that broken identity is often rebuilt in private before it shows up in public. It taught me that God is too faithful to let us stay where He never intended us to live.

If you are reading this and you are beginning again, you are not starting from scratch; you are starting from experience. God has not abandoned you. You are not too broken, too late, too lost, or too far gone. What fell apart needed to fall. What you survived did not take you out because purpose is still attached to your name.

Your story probably began with pain, but it will end with God's promise. This is the chapter where God makes all things new!

Chapter 9
Author- Ebony Jefferson
"HOW TO WAR"

The practical and the spiritual

How to combat unspoken expectations, division, and poor communication?

- <u>**Communicate your needs and desires.**</u> No one reads minds and should not be expected to do so.
- <u>**Have those hard conversations.**</u> Be sure that it is done in a tone that your partner is receptive to and do it in private.
- <u>**Never allow anyone to come between you and your spouse, even if you are upset with one another.**</u> My ex-husband felt that when we had conflicts, he no longer had to respect me or the boundaries and the privacy of our marriage. He would uncover me and our marriage in the worst ways. And he thought this behavior was okay

because we were upset with each other at the moment. I later realized just how much this had imprinted on my heart and mind, and at times, it felt like emotional abuse and abandonment. In his mind, the respect in our marriage did not have to be upheld. This spiraled into other unhealthy behaviors and patterns. This kind of behavior is the worst thing that you can do to your partner. The two of you are one flesh; you are to operate as one. Men are to be the head of the household. They are the priest of the home. They are to ***love their wives as Christ loves the church. He gave up his life for her***. **(Ephesians 5:25)**

- ***Social media, family, and friends should never know your private and personal matters in your marriage.*** It is okay to have one or two individuals that you and your spouse have agreed to confide in for wisdom, advice, and clarity, but outside of that, you should not be discussing your private matters. I do not recommend that those people be family. Keep others out of your personal business. You really should be taking everything to God in prayer, but there is safety in the counsel of wisdom from appointed and trusted sources.

- ***Never become stiff-necked, unteachable, disrespectful, and stubborn.*** It will destroy a marriage faster than you know. Be wise as serpents but harmless as doves. (Matthew 10:16)
- ***Kill pride, lust, and selfishness.*** No marriage will last when these spirits are at work. You must destroy them before they destroy you and your marriage.
- ***Never express in your actions or use your mouth to tear your husband down, or allow anyone else to.*** Instead, use your words and spiritual authority in the spirit to build your home. Through a lifestyle of prayer and fasting. Marriage requires spiritual warfare because the one who desires to cause division in your home is not flesh and

blood. Your spouse is not your enemy; satan is. The two of you fight him together.

- <u>**Marriage requires togetherness, patience, and a plan of action.**</u> You and your spouse must develop a system for avoiding cycles of unhealthy behaviors and patterns. There must be a plan of action that combats patterns that are not fruitful in the marriage. Every case is not the same; this is where you and your spouse can explore the best options that work for your marriage. The two of you must write a vision! Let him lead, and you follow.
- Although we desire for all that are married to remain married and allow God to restore your covenant, God is not requiring anyone to remain an abusive marriage or one that has been defiled by cheating. Make sure that you have biblical grounds for a divorce so that you do not end up committing adultery. Find out what the Bible deems acceptable and not acceptable.

Remember, "what God joins together let no one put asunder." Often times we forget to consult God, but he should be our priority.

Think higher!

I was watching a reel the other day, and one of the hosts on the show was a single female who is dating. She mentioned her boyfriend and shared that the sexual intimacy between her and her boyfriend was better than she had ever experienced, and rated his love based on that and a few other things. I want to say this to the women who are not yet married: having sex with a man who is not your husband is not a flex. It is a huge red flag. Why? Because this man cares NOTHING about your soul. He does not fear God. He has no control over his sexual appetite, and that means there is no conviction to stop him from cheating, abusing, misusing, and abandoning you. He is only after what gratifies his flesh in the moment. There are so many things that transpire during sex that lead to things like soul-ties and more. This earth is not eternal; there is an immediate destination after this.

You need a husband who understands priesthood! One who fears God too much to defile your temple and cause you to fall into temptation. Therefore, pray that God gives your husband vision & purpose, and the two of you can begin cultivating that as you are waiting.

It is so important that we do the necessary work to make sure we enter into a marriage healthy, whole, and healed. And let me be clear, that journey is not pretty. At the spiritual altar of the Lord, is where we allow things in us to die that do not serve or honor God. In my time of singleness, there was so much that the Lord had to process in me that could make me suitable and compatible for His son. I was mean, I physically and psychologically abused when I did not get my way.

I was immature and irresponsible with my words and actions when I was not treated properly. Even if it seems like those things were warranted, and at times they were, they never fixed anything. In fact, it made things worse. As we were preparing to write this book, I heard the Holy Spirit tell me, "Things are going to be different because you are different." So my prayer became, teach me, Holy Spirit, how to be a wise wife!

Here's how: Speak life in EVERY situation. NEVER speak what you see but speak what you want to see! Speak life into your marriage, your man, your children, your finances, and your business.

God did not give Adam options. He gave Adam purpose, and when purpose was established, here came Eve. Formed out of Adam's rib to help him carry out the plans of God. I want you to notice how the enemy showed up immediately when Eve was created. We see no evidence of him with just Adam. satan understands agreement, so as soon as they became husband and wife, he appeared. Be armed and ready to war against the enemy. That's why it is necessary to do the work before marriage, so you do not spend time fighting each other, but the real enemy.

Where there is a lack of forgiveness and sin, spiritual warfare enters. Kill every Jezebel & Ahab spirit. There must be proper order in the home. The woman must submit, and the husband must lead. Women do not stifle, manipulate, or control your spouses. If it has been going on, sis, you are out of order. The Bible says that the two of you are to be submitting one to another out of reverence for Christ. (Ephesians 5:21)

Nothing is honorable about being dominary and controlling. While the anointing is attractive and gifts are without repentance, it does not mean a person possesses the character, integrity, and capacity required to steward a marriage. It is possible to master some areas and completely fail in others. Think about your favorite subject in school, and then think about your least favorite. When in relationships and especially to have longevity in marriage, it matters who you are as a person, beyond the ordination, titles, and positions. As mentioned earlier, the divorce rates of spiritual leaders are just as high. Indicating a false balance or poor preparation. Pre-marital counseling, deliverance, and money management are mandatory. Love covers all flaws, but it does not pay bills, it does not cause demons to flee. There are some spiritual as well as practical things that we must do in order to sustain and have a healthy, happy marriage. While the anointing is attractive and gifts are without repentance, it does not mean a person possesses the character, integrity, and capacity required to steward a marriage. It is possible to master some areas and completely fail in others. Think about your favorite subject in school, and then think about your least favorite. When in relationships and especially to have longevity in marriage, it matters who you are as a person, beyond the ordination, titles, and positions.

    As mentioned earlier, the divorce rates of spiritual leaders are just as high. Indicating a false balance or poor preparation. Pre-marital counseling, deliverance, and money management are mandatory. Love covers all flaws, but it does not pay bills, it does not cause demons to flee. There are some spiritual as well as practical things that we must do in order to sustain and have a healthy, happy marriage. The problem is that most people equate and automatically couple "gifted" with "integral".

"Anointing" with "good character", but the truth is, they are developed individually.

Discernment can peel back those layers that are often very attractive when at work, but discernment helps reveal the truth. Where an individual cannot hide behind the call, and the anointing and discernment allow you to see that their character, maturity level, and integrity may or may not align with or meet the standard. You may desire to court and marry a person, but you may not have the capacity to steward their destiny, your destiny, and anything else that comes with that. Discernment works on the anointed and the called, too. So a person can spot the red flags in you, even though you can preach, prophecy, and exhort heaven down. And we cannot see red flags in ourselves and other people, and behave as if we are at a carnival. We must address them early on to avoid conflict down the road. I am a person who needs to be assured that you carry sustaining power, or does your strength grow small in adversity? Do you break down the moment things get hard? Who or what do you run to? When an individual has been in tough positions before, they gain wisdom, clarity, and hindsight to better navigate the future.

In today's time, when you are not easily manipulated, you are labeled crazy, unsubmissive, or even degrading. Some of us can see past gifts and anointing and can see the broken, wounded, unreliable person a person presently is, and realize we are not saviors. No one is responsible for your healing but you. Marrying potential is the worst decision anyone can make because not everyone desires to reach that potential, and then you are stuck in their complacency. And that's not fair to anyone, especially someone who has done the work and who is healed. I saw a social media reel that said, "A lot of people are experiencing unhealthy limerence. That is when you are addicted to people that do not choose you. It is when your trauma chooses your partner. Inconsistency feels like home! If someone makes you feel more anxious than consistency that is your childhood wound begging for closure. You are not a rehabilitation center for badly raised men and vice versa. It is not your job to fix them, raise them, or change them. You want a partner, not a project. You want a prayer partner and not them only being prayer points. You want a priest who understands priesthood and a submissive woman who respects her husband!!

Chapter 10
Author- Ebony Jefferson
"THE ALTAR"

Have you ever truly wondered why the wedding ceremony traditionally takes place at the altar? Or why it is even called a ceremony. Or why we take vows to and make covenants one to another. When searching the meaning of these terms, they are all spiritual and not physical. And many people do not know this, which is why the Bible cautions us not to enter into marriage lightly. (1 Corinthians 7) So why is it that we start a spiritual matter but do not understand that we will have to engage in spiritual warfare and utilize spiritual weapons to sustain it?

When you study the Bible, scripture shows us that an altar is how the spiritual realm transacts with the natural realm for both good and evil. In the Old Testament, the priest used physical altars, sacrificing animals to atone for sin, because Jesus Christ had not come yet to die for our sins. This was God's system that He temporarily instructed the priest to do until Jesus came. Although it was not enough to rid the guilt of sin and pay the price like Christ's death, it was temporarily sufficient for God. But why? Why must there be sacrifices on the altar before the Lord? Because sin carries a wage. The wages of sin are death, death entered when Adam and Eve disobeyed God; we were never meant to live a life of sin and death. Every time someone encountered God's presence or went to sacrifice, the bible would say, "There they built an altar unto the Lord..."

There was also Balaam, who built altars for King Balak to curse God's chosen people, Israel. King Balak saw how powerful the army of Israel was compared to his army and understood they could not defeat them naturally/physically, so in fear, he concluded that he would defeat them spiritually by raising altars to curse them. (Numbers chapters 22-24) And believe it or not, this is still happening today, especially in churches and in marriages. Not everyone has the heart of God, and some people are inwardly hoping for the downfall of others and will do whatever it takes to see you fall. Do not be deceived or naive. The lives of Joseph, Job, David, and more should prove that you have to be covered, and your marriage is no different. By now, you may be wondering why I am speaking of altars and what does that have to do with marriage. Hang on, the Holy Spirit will tie this all together shortly.

Fire Must Continuously Be Burning On The Altar!

The altar is not only meant for sacrifices, but it's also the place where covenants are established. I have heard several people say that they have read the entire Bible, but if you are not reading the word of God for it to become one with you, and if you are not reading the word of God for this to become life unto you, then it is in vain. Jada Pinkett Smith and Lizzo have both said that they have read the entire Bible. Jada Pickett Smith also said, "She still do not know God." You cannot read the word of God, trying to figure God out. The human mind cannot even began to grasp the level of high intelligence and brilliance that the divine creater is. God is a spirit, His kingdom is a spirit, you must approach and even worship Him in spirit and in truth and will your whole heart and not just your mind. Our confession of faith during salvation are not just words but a covenant between you and God likened unto a marriage. (Matthew chapters 22-23)

The altar is not a pretty place.

The altar is not just a physical thing that is designed to look pretty. In fact, there are some qualifications that must be met to carry out the transaction for good or evil. There is order at the altar, specific instructions would be given by the Holy Spirit for good and by an evil spirit for bad! In the Bible, Aaron, who was Moses' brother, a prophet and priest, and he had two sons. He was a part of the Levitical priests, a very special tribe in Israel that was set aside for God's specific use. One day, Aaron's son went to offer up a sacrifice in the temple, but they used the wrong incense, they did not follow the order of God, and the Bible says they died at the altar. God did not play about the temple, and He still does not, but Jesus has ushered in grace that abounds, but there is order and must be reference.

Exchange

The altar is the place of exchange. It is the place that we stand before our loved ones and God to make a commitment and vows, but it is also the spiritual place that we must return to daily to die a spiritual death of the flesh. The altar is the place that we allow God to ALTER us into His image and likeness so that our marriage can reflect His intention and design. At a physical altar, things do not just die, they are slaughtered!! The altar is bloody. It smells. Blood is draining because something is being exchanged for something else. On our spiritual altar, as the flesh dies, we are exchanging stubbornness for a broken and contrite spirit. We are exchanging and killing pride so that our hearts are not hardened towards our spouses.

The Ultimate Sacrifice

Jesus became the ultimate sacrifice and paid the price for sin. He was beaten, bruised, bloody, and hung. He did not die for your salvation alone; He died for your covenant with God and your covenant with your spouse. You, your spouse, and God are 3 chords that cannot easily be broken because of His SACRIFICE upon the altar! Although we no longer need or use physical altars as believers, there are spiritual altars that we are to raise before the Lord and keep them burning with prayer, supplication, worship, and praise that create atmospheres for the spirit of God to come and abide. As declared in the Old Testament, sacrifices on the altar of the Lord come before God as a sweet aroma, and that is still true today. We are living sacrifices that are to be holy and acceptable unto God. (Romans 12:1)

Honor the Lord with your marriage. Give it to Him. Make it a priority between the two of you to continue allowing the flesh to die on the altar so that your marriage can live. The moment either of you abandons the place of the altar, you abandon and uncover the marriage, making it an open target for the enemy to come in. Always stay in a posture of a servant, one to another and unto God. If you have gotten out of alignment, repent quickly and follow God's command. Study the word and fast together often and do it more together than separately. There is power in agreement, and this is why you will experience spiritual warfare in your marriage because satan hates unity. Again, satan did not appear in scripture with Adam alone; he appeared when Eve arrived. He is all about division, to divide and conquer. Why? Because together you pose a bigger threat. One can chase a thousand demons, and two— ten thousand. When you war together, you are literally causing God to push back the darkness, and the Lord will raise a standard against the enemy.

Always keep in mind, and I know we say it, but we have to be careful when we say, "The Lord said..." Remember, the Holy Spirit is not causing division, pinning people against each other, or causing strife in the marriage. Lastly, men, instead of trying to change your wife into who you want her to be, help her become the woman God needs and created her to be, and she will become the wife you want, and the same for you wives. You cannot change him, but God most certainly can as long as he is willing to allow the Lord to work on him. Also, you should not control, manipulate, or force anybody to be something that you also are not. You should be what you require in most situations. When the head of the household is out of alignment, he causes the home to be out of alignment.

Always remember, every time you complain about your" spouse, your heart hardens toward them. Every time you pray for your spouse, your heart softens.

I speak life over you and your spouse that as you both submit to each other and Christ, you possess the inheritance and land, a land flowing with milk and honey, while being fruitful and multiplying! When you see no fruit of these things, seriously fast and pray. Be the violent one who comes to take it by force. (Matthew 11:12)

God Bless!

The EbonyJ Brand
Publishing Services

Serves as an umbrella for
Publishing, Real Estate, Fashion, and Ministry.

For publishing services

Contact: details@theebonyjbrand.com

www.ingramcontent.com/pod-product-compliance
Lightning Source LLC
Chambersburg PA
CBHW060823190426
43197CB00038B/2201